Peace Studies

Peace Studies

Toward a Transformative Perspective

by
Karuna Maddava

LEPS Press
DeKalb, Illinois
LEPS Press, Northern Illinois University
DeKalb, Illinois 60115

© 1994 by LEPS Press. All rights reserved.
Published in 1994
Printed in the United States of America

Managing Editor: Caryn Rudy
Copy Editor: Bruce Woll
Cover Art Director: Mary Lou Read-Dreyer
Cover Illustration: Katrina Elisa Davis-Salazar

Distributed by LEPS Press

Library of Congress Catalog-in-Publication Data

Maddava, Karuna A.
   Peace studies : toward a transformative perspective / by Karuna A. Maddava.
      p.   cm.
   Includes Index.
   ISBN 1-879528-10-X
   1. Peace—Study and teaching—United States. I. Title.
   JX1904.M33   1994
   327.1'72'071173—dc20   94-12330
                                            CIP

Figure 1, page 7, reproduced by permission of Routledge.

Dedication

To Henry, for watering my seeds.

"Peace is not a subject to be studied and discussed but never lived. It should be disturbing to each student. It should unsettle all one's notions about politics, about possible careers, about life-style itself. It should be impossible for anyone who participates in a peace studies program to again see the world in the same way."
—Wehr and Washburn
Peace and World Order Studies

"Some people might start exploring the foundations of peace research and end up going deeper and deeper into the matter until they disappear and are not heard from ever again."
—Johan Galtung

"There never was a war that was not inward; I must fight till I have conquered in myself what causes war."
—Marianne Moore
"In Distrust of Merits"

Contents

List of Figures ix
List of Appendices xi
Foreword xiii
Preface xvii
Acknowledgements xix
1. Historical Overview of Peace Studies 1
2. Ideologies of Peace Studies 15
3. A Liberationist Critique 55
4. Toward a Transformationist Approach 69
5. A Review of Peace Studies Programs 99
6. Curricular Implications of the Transformationist Approach . . 129
Appendices 145
Bibliography 153
Index 169

Figures

1. Defining Peace 7
2. The Three Representative Educational Ideologies in Peace Studies 22
3. Map 103
4. Examples of Representative Peace Studies Programs 104

Appendices

A. Peace Studies Journal 147
B. Questionnaire 149
C. Emphasis or Focus of Peace Studies, Graph 151

Foreword

As a symbolic event, Desert Storm seemed a final rejoinder to anti-war and peace activism. The Post-Viet Nam blues were over now Americans were told. It was time for the nation to settle into its place at the pinnacle of a new world order as the first truly global military power. We could organize the international police-keeping responsibilities necessary to ensure access to the resources that meant American jobs. We didn't even need nuclear weapons. As a means to maintain the prerequisite order for international trade, war had apparently been rehabilitated as a respectable policy instrument.

This bravado hardly outlasted the war. It turned out that progress toward the ordering of life—personal, cultural, political, and even international—had little to do with military prowess. The ensuing sense of chaos still awaits a broad conversation about the conditions from which genuine orderliness in human relationship might be sustained. The discussants in such conversations have so far been few, the representatives of violent reactivity, many. In the short time since the Gulf War, simple place names have become a sort of index to the evils of our times—the World Trade Center, Somalia, Los Angeles, Rwanda, and Bosnia. At home, it is the names of obscure persons which quickly become the powerful bearers of a whole culture's pain and confusion—Rodney King, Reginald Denny, and Lorenna Bobbitt. The fear-based focus on violence and the means for suppressing it leaves little room for talk about peace.

Only a transformed education can generate the conversation about the meaning and conditions of peace, certainly the only conditions of lasting order. Though public education will ultimately be central to any such effort, it is not to the primary school, but to the college and university that we must first turn. These institutions still retain the leverage and critical traditions necessary to move opinion in many public arenas. As yet we still do not have a firm grasp on what has already been achieved in the systematic study of peace in higher education programs. We know little about the underlying premises, ideological commitments, and methods used in investigating peace. We don't even know how "peace" is understood in all the varieties of peace studies efforts.

Karuna Maddava's analysis here of the philosophical and political commitments of peace studies programs in the United States is an important contribution to scholars in the field of Peace Studies and to all those seeking to grasp the main lines of argument in a vast literature. She identifies (1) the underlying liberal premises which ground most peace studies programs today, (2) provides critiques of these positions from what she terms broadly the liberationist and transformationist perspectives, and (3) argues for the traces and curricular implications of the transformative approach.

This book is a revision of a Master's Thesis in Educational Foundations at Northern Illinois University, completed in 1991—before all the events cited above had reshaped our collective sense of social reality. In 1992, the thesis earned Karuna Maddava the Outstanding Scholarship Award granted annually by the Department of Leadership and Educational Policy Studies. In its present form, the study remains a unique analysis, even more timely than when it was first drafted. In it the working premises of the Peace Studies movement in higher education are clarified and criticized. But this is more than an analytical work. Maddava has succeeded in forming the intellectual bases for a new direction in Peace Studies curriculum. This thoughtful work is exemplary of the kind of reflective educational practice capable of implementing both the vision and the methods toward a transformed world.

    Wilma Miranda
    6 June 1994

Preface

We all have critical junctures in our lives--times when we encounter someone or something that changes the direction of our lives. My journey into peace studies began long before I realized, on a sunny college campus. As a first generation college student, my goals were set: a large diamond ring, fur coat, sports car, and lots of money. I stepped into what I thought was going to be an introduction to sociology class with a three-inch-thick textbook. Just one more class to get me on my way to comfortable living. Instead, a wise and gentle man sat with us in a circle and introduced us to critical, radical analyses, eastern philosophy, and the existential questions of humankind. My mind took off like a rocket on a path I could not have envisioned.

The passage into adulthood is not an easy thing. We question, ruminate, as we attempt to find our place and purpose in life. This passage for me, as with so many, was particularly difficult. I thought for the first time. Really thought. And questioned. This tumultuous time culminated with me throwing off five years of full-time study in an area I had come to realize I could not, in good conscience, work in. Throwing off this yoke left me so light, I felt I could do anything. I could step back and truthfully ask, "If I could do anything, what would I do?" After much thought and inquiry, the answer came: peace studies.

I came to the field with a thirst for peace theory and action. For anyone who hopes for justice and human rights for all people, for having their basic needs met, for ending violence and transforming relationships, no field holds as much wisdom and promise as the field of peace studies. The ways in which peace studies can help to transform violence at personal, interpersonal, group, societal, national, and international levels are astounding. I was drunk with the possibility of change.

After more than two years of researching the field, I sobered up. While much was being accomplished, the majority of peace studies research, theory, and education clearly was maintaining the status quo. The liberal ideological base representative of most of the field promotes change, but within the existing system. Deep-cutting analyses of structural violence and guidelines for how we can bring peace into our daily lives were rare. An analysis of peace studies programs paralleled the overwhelmingly liberal ideological base of the literature. This study is an attempt to uncover and analyze the ideological bases of peace studies research and education, and to point to and explore critical analyses which may lead the field into a more influential future.

Acknowledgements

I would like to thank the following people for their extraordinary patience, faith, and support in this effort: my husband, Henry Beardsley, who made this effort possible; my parents, Don and Kathy Lundstrom, for unconditional love; my best friend, Brian O'Keefe Spruill, who kept me laughing and thinking; my thesis commitee, Sherman Stanage, Richard Quinney, and Wilma Miranda, for mentoring, inspiration, and unending patience; and editor, Phyllis Cunningham, for brutal honesty.

1. Historical Overview of Peace Studies

The quest for peace expresses a universal human desire that has and will always exist. "Carl Jung refers to peace as an archetype that exists within the collective unconscious. According to him and others, all people desire peace and social justice" (Harris 1988, 56). It seems natural to want peace, yet fighting and war have plagued humanity for millennia. Why? Love of power? Greed? Scarcity of resources? Or could it be the sheer excitement and power of war itself? These questions, among myriad others, underlie our quest for peace.

Peace education efforts in the United States began well before the first World War. These efforts, mostly at the elementary school level, were an outgrowth of the strong peace movement early in this century. These were characterized by "good citizenship, or world citizenship" education rather than peace education (Harris 1988, 44). As might be expected, peace education efforts rose in reactions to World War I (WWI) and World War II (WWII). However, they remained an extension of international relations. It was in the 1940s that some researchers in traditional fields, such as mathematician/sociologist Johan Galtung, shifted the focus of discussion from war to the nature of peace. This was a significant intellectual step that helped pave the way for the development of peace studies as a new discipline. Though it may be argued that peace movements have arisen over many centuries, peace studies as a formalized field in higher education dates from 1948 in the United States. Peace researcher George Lopez divides the history of university-level peace studies programs into three distinct time periods: "[1] the formative years of the mid-1960s through the early 1970s; [2] the institutionalization of peace studies from the mid-1970s to the early 1980s; and [3] the era dominated by nuclear education and the challenge of specialization in conflict resolution, which began in the early 1980s and continues to the present" (1989b, 62). As may be expected, peace studies programs were often created in response to war, or conflict. The first university-level programs appeared after World War II.

It is not surprising that when the devastation and destruction of WWII was fully comprehended, it fostered a response from the new field of peace studies. The first formal peace studies program was instituted in 1948 at Manchester College in Indiana, a Brethren-affiliated liberal arts school. The next program did not come for another eight years, when in 1955 the Center for Conflict Resolution was started at the University of Michigan under the guidance of Elise and Kenneth

Boulding (Lopez 1989b, 63). These programs, however, were ahead of their time. The spread of peace studies was slow, and it was not accepted as a formal, institutionalized field for another ten to fifteen years. In fact, it took another major war to do it.

The Vietnam War changed the face of this nation, fueling raging debates and conflicts here at home. For the first time, not only a particular war, but war itself was being challenged by unprecedented numbers of people. Many U.S. peace studies programs came into being during or after the Vietnam War as universities attempted to respond to the challenges of public debate over the war. These programs varied in focus and scope. Since many of these early programs were created in response to war, it is not surprising that most of their curricula, at least in the early years, focused on prevention of war and alternative methods of resolving disputes between countries. The Vietnam War, then, institutionalized peace studies in our universities.

The next phase in the development of peace studies brought about branches or specializations within the broader field. As the nuclear arsenals multiplied in the seventies and early eighties, the public became increasingly concerned with the arms race and the possibility of nuclear war. With the immense proliferation of nuclear weapons, anti-nuclear groups sprang up across the country. Peace educators responded by expanding their research and teaching efforts devoted specifically to nuclear issues. In fact, so much energy was channeled into research and writing on nuclear issues, that, since the sixties, approximately a third of the literature is solely devoted to nuclear studies.

The tremendous increase of information and analysis in the area of nuclear issues alone created a distinct new branch of peace education. Many consider it an entirely separate field of study. This is also the case with conflict studies. The late seventies and early eighties saw a rise in the interest and material on conflict resolution and negotiation, pioneered by the Bouldings at the University of Michigan in 1955. Conflict resolution programs are still thriving, and although closely tied to peace studies, they, too, are autonomous enough to be considered a separate subset of peace studies. One can think of these two fields being related to peace studies as international relations is to political science, or criminology to sociology. Nuclear studies and conflict studies are the two largest branches of peace studies.

While some peace studies programs focus almost exclusively on nuclear studies or conflict resolution, many programs combine several aspects of studying peace, as well as integrating it into daily life. Though the eighties saw the development of these two main branches of peace studies, even more noteworthy was the increase in the number of programs.

Wehr and Washburn, in *Peace and World Order Systems* counted 60 undergraduate and 26 graduate programs in the U.S. in 1976. The fifth edition of *Peace and World Order Studies: A Curriculum Guide* (Thomas and Klare 1989), cites over 180 undergraduate programs, 38 graduate programs, and an additional 150 institutions in the U.S. as offering some course in peace studies. David Cianto, in COPRED's (Consortium for Peace Research, Education, and Development) 1990 study, cites 185 programs in the U.S. Another figure, possibly including non-degree granting programs, describes the U.S. as having 235 peace studies programs as of 1987 (Harris 1988, 44). Also of significance, beyond the great proliferation of programs, are two important events in the history of peace studies.

The first was the founding of COPRED in 1970. Its purpose is to "promote the expansion and integration of peace research, peace education, and peace action in North America, and to act as a liaison with the International Peace Research Association (IPRA), which promotes similar functions in other parts of the world" (Harris 1988, 42). COPRED sponsors the journal, *Peace and Change*, and acts as a clearinghouse for information on peace studies.

The second significant event took place in 1984, when Congress passed legislation that founded the U.S. Institute of Peace (USIP). The purpose of the Institute is "research, [sponsoring peace research projects,] education and training, and information services, or public education" (Sweeney 1984, 154). USIP has since awarded many grants for research, publication, and curriculum development (Thomas 1987, 10). Although the history of formalized peace studies is a short one, we can recognize landmarks and stages in its development, while watching the history that is being forged and created today.

The Quest for Definition

To discuss peace, analyze peace studies programs, and, ultimately, create a peace studies program, one is confronted with a daunting task—defining peace. The first, and foremost, problem when discussing peace is "what is it?" The term itself is disputed, and at times, an empty construct. There are as many different definitions as there are peace researchers, scholars, and activists. To begin discussing peace, we must look at the constellations of meaning as used by activists, educators, and researchers. How is the term "peace" used and understood?

Though scholars have many differing definitions of peace, most of them recognize the distinction made by Johan Galtung between negative and positive peace, where negative peace is the absence of war. Examples of efforts to achieve negative peace are the arms race, anti-nuclear arguments, and Middle Eastern or Central American conflict studies. Negative peace efforts focus on the present and near future, and on immediate or potential physical threats; it attempts to eliminate the conditions that generate the threats. Negative peace gets its name by being particularly concerned with reactively eradicating existing problems and tensions, rather than proactively dealing with potential problems and installing good and just relations and conditions.

Positive peace efforts have more far reaching and future oriented agendas. These involve a reordering of global priorities to promote social justice, environmental preservation, economic development, and participatory political processes. It is an attempt to reconstruct conditions toward a more humane, just world. Positive peace proponents hope to create future attitudes that would ultimately make negative peace efforts obsolete. Examples of positive peace recommendations are meeting basic needs for all humans, focusing on service, and realizing the interconnectedness of life (the global village). To really wage peace and change the world, we must move into positive peace making.

In attempting to define peace, there seems to be a widespread acceptance of the Galtungian term "structural violence," which he defines as the "unintended harm done to human beings, as a process, working slowly as the way misery in general, and hunger in particular, erode and finally kill human beings" (Galtung 1985, 145). Direct violence is intended, and therefore is usually quick and obvious. However, some of the main structures of society have characteristics that inherently harm people. In such a setting, an individual may be doing enormous harm to other individuals without his or her knowledge or intention, which is structural violence.

Figure 1. Defining Peace

```
                          Violence
              ┌──────────────────────────────┐
              ▼                              ▼
          DIRECT                         INDIRECT
          VIOLENCE                       VIOLENCE
       Personal e.g. assault,         Structural e.g. poverty
         riot, terrorism, war         hunger, discrimination,
                                            apartheid
              │                              │
              ▼                              ▼
          Absence of                     Absence of
       personal violence              structural violence
              or                              or
        NEGATIVE PEACE                  POSITIVE PEACE
              ▲                              ▲
              └──────────────────────────────┘
                           Peace
```

David Hicks incorporates direct and structural violence in his graph for defining peace (1988, 6).

Many peace studies scholars agree that direct and structural violence should be included when defining peace, and that with such a definition, a focus on justice naturally emerges:

Birgit Brock-Utne:

[A] broad definition of peace includes such factors as the distribution of wealth within states . . . the absence of direct violence and the absence of indirect or structural violence . . . [and] that every human being regardless of sex has the right to a life of peace (the UN declaration of 1978) and peace is defined as justice, the right to fulfillment of basic needs, to self-determination . . . (1985, 1-3).

Michael Howard:

[Peace is] the bringing together [of] the two coordinates of order and justice. . . . How much injustice are we prepared to tolerate in the interest of order, and how much disorder do we regard as legitimate to provoke in the interest of justice (Kaye 1987, 4)?

The National Council of Churches:

Peace is a world in which neither the overt violence of war nor the covert violence of unjust systems is used as an instrument for extending the interests of a particular nation or group. It is a world where basic human needs are met, and in which justice can be obtained and conflict resolved through nonviolent processes and human and material resources are shared for the benefit of all people (Thomas and Klare 1989, 38).

Though it has been "defined" hundreds of times, peace remains a controversial term, particularly when it includes concepts of justice, which people define differently. Johan Galtung sees this as positive:

I think we shall never come to anything like a final conclusion as to what "peace" might mean. Nor do I think we should ever hope for that to happen: The moment we arrive at a consensus within, and even without, the peace research community as to the meaning of "peace," the basis is already laid for the ossification of peace research and practice and the creation of one more technocratic production line, presumably producing peace. Rather, I think it is our task to continue to draw on the richness of that concept in the geography and history of civilization and culture, exploring more and more facets of that diamond (1988, 246).

Tensions brought about by the disagreements over definition are often welcomed and viewed as desirable. "Antagonisms insure that the dialectic is kept alive" (Folk 1978, 59).

In relation to peace education, there is a wide range of questions: Who or what controls the definition of peace and peaceful processes? How is it to be defined in a curricular context? Who is "qualified" to teach peace? Peace is used in many different ways by peace educators; there is not widespread agreement on what it is they are teaching. It is no wonder, then, that with this plethora of "challenges," peace studies is not readily accepted as an area of study or discipline.

Overview of Peace Education Efforts: Assets and Problems

Peace studies, like other "emerging" fields such as African-American studies, women's studies, or Latino studies, is far from being accepted as a discipline. Like almost any new field, peace studies is seen as creating an even greater drain on already limited institutional financial resources. It is also viewed by some as lacking a sound historical, intellectual base. We must ask the question, "On whose shoulders is peace studies standing?"

Peace studies, as mentioned earlier, initially came out of the field of international relations. However, one could say that peace studies uses or borrows methods of research from almost all major disciplines found in the liberal arts tradition. Peace studies stands on the shoulders of history, political science, philosophy, education, sociology, physics, biology, psychology, communications, English, and law, among other disciplines and fields of inquiry. Peace research uses empirical and normative methods, and has its disputes and competing paradigms, as does any discipline. The field of peace studies has no less than fifteen scholarly journals specifically devoted to peace issues (see Appendix A). Although the roots of peace studies lie in parent disciplines, it must necessarily be multidisciplinary, with a unique subject matter and style. Nigel Young provides a succinct definition of peace studies as separate and distinct from other fields: "Peace studies is studying positive and negative peace, violent and non-violent conflict, physical and structural violence, conflict resolution and peaceful cooperation, creative and destructive social change, applied to the individual, interpersonal, societal, national, and international levels" (1987, 31).

Peace studies is in no way "non-academic"; in this day and age, it is a crucial aspect of study for any institution of higher learning. Peace studies in its policy analysis dimension addresses the most pressing issues of our time. "Peace studies must be portrayed—and unfold in fact—as wrestling with the most important and difficult issues of the day" (Mulch 1989, 83). One reason some critics of peace studies programs view them as non-academic is the belief that peace studies is simply indoctrination. Rather, it is grounded in critical study of social/personal conditions.

Peace educators must emphasize this critical function of their work. Much of the effort in academic settings is to teach the critical and analytical skills needed to test some of the most powerful myths of the society. Ultimately, we must realize that nothing can be taught from a "non-ideological" standpoint. Teaching is infused with the values of the teachers. "Peace education is not aimed at indoctrination . . . rather, a key element in peace education is 'good educational practice': adherence to the fostering of skills of analysis and reasoning, research, and evaluation which are common to most disciplined fields of inquiry" (Burns 1987, 39).

It cannot be denied that peace education does come from a value base—that of valuing peace; however, it does not follow that peace education has no place in the school. After all, what discipline does not involve values? Every judgment made—what book to use, how to teach, assignments given—and so on, involves values, however subtle. Peace studies is analogous to the field of medicine: peace studies values peace and tries to bring about peace while eliminating violence and war, while medicine values and tries to bring about health while eliminating sickness and disease.

The most difficult hurdle for peace educators, however, is also the most obvious—that of simple knowledge. If peace educators are to create a "science" of peace to respond to the highly developed science of war, they must counter with knowledge, judgment, and skill, as well as a knack for sharing this knowledge with students in a democratic and participatory fashion. An educator must master a vast amount of knowledge in such varied fields as sociology, international relations, conflict studies, anthropology, literature, philosophy, and history, to name a few. The sheer scope of peace studies can be overwhelming. And since peace studies is such a new discipline, the majority of the people teaching in it come from their primary academic disciplines to peace studies, many or most of them having no specific training in peace. As more educators are trained in the actual study of peace, and become knowledgeable in these many areas, the face of peace studies in our schools could change.

Though peace studies faces some large obstacles, we must give credit to the fact that what peace educators are attempting to do is perhaps the most noble of causes—to teach peace, to promote global peace and understanding, to raise the level of justice and harmony, to raise consciousness itself, possibly, even, to save the earth and all things on it. This is no small undertaking. What better cause could engage a teacher's time? Unlike many educators, the peace educator is touching matters that are directly relevant to student's lives. Students do worry about nuclear holocaust, they suffer from personal conflict, and they worry about loved ones who fight in wars. "Why should teachers turn their backs on this turmoil and teach as if it didn't exist, ignoring student's real concerns over the way violence and militarism impact on their lives" (Harris 1988, 80)? Peace studies has the potential to address real life problems for students in areas and in ways left untouched by other disciplines. It provides a forum for open discussion on the toughest of issues, and serves to inform them about the most pressing concerns of the day.

Overview of Chapters 2 Through 6

Chapter 2 is an overview of the ideologies found in the literature of peace studies: liberalism, liberationism, and transformationism. I discuss the relationship of the political and epistemological underpinnings of these ideologies, and the common thread running through all of them—democracy and democratization. The search covers the work of several recognized peace studies educators and scholars, such as Betty Reardon, Elise Boulding, and Johan Galtung, among others. I explore the differing patterns and perspectives on peace studies through the historic struggles and transformation of the field and ask: What are the common concerns, the main topics, peace scholars are addressing? What are the main disagreements? What underlying patterns are visible in their work? and Where does peace studies seem to be going from here?

In Chapter 3, I examine direct and structural violence from a liberationist perspective, which provides a very powerful critique. I address the topics of just war, patriarchy, and capitalism and ask: What are the main institutions of structural violence in our society? What philosophical, political, and economic beliefs underlie these institutions? and How can we change forms of structural violence in order to bring about a more peaceful society?

Chapter 4 brings the critique from a social/institutional to a personal level. After having reviewed the literature and programs, recurring problems and limitations arose in the main philosophical and political approaches to peace studies. The theory presented in Chapter 4 addresses those problems and provides a new, alternative perspective on peace and peace studies. I develop a critical epistemology focusing on being peace and based in the transformationist approach. The personal philosophy of peace that emerges proposes an alternative way of looking at and studying peace.

Chapter 5 describes and discusses current peace studies programs in higher education in the U.S. The search covers programs that grant either a minor, a Bachelor's or a Graduate Degree directly in peace studies, or with an emphasis in peace studies. I examine these programs from several perspectives. First, a historical/statistically descriptive analysis is carried out: When was the program started, and under what context? What are the number of peace studies courses available through these programs, the number of courses required for a degree in peace studies, or for an emphasis in peace studies? Is the program interdisciplinary, or is it housed within a department? In what and how many subject areas are the peace studies courses offered? What areas are focused on or targeted by each program? What are these peace studies students actually studying? The ideological base of each program varies, which each curriculum reflects. Some schools are pragmatically grounded, others are spiritual. Some include dozens of subject areas; others, only a few. This perspective for analysis is the main portion of discussion, as it provides the actual subject matter taught and learned in the field of peace studies.

Having examined current peace studies programs, I then look at the curricular implications of the critical epistemology presented in Chapter 4. In Chapter 4, I argue that transformationism is the most complete and promising of the three ideologies in peace studies. In Chapter 6, I ask, What are the characteristics of transformationist peace education? If one could design an 'ideal' peace studies major from a transformationist approach, what would it be? The book, then, takes us through the literature, ideologies, programs, and curricular implications of peace studies in the United States.

2. Ideologies of Peace Studies

To understand the philosophical and political foundations of peace studies, we must ask certain questions: How has the field of peace studies developed conceptually over time? What are the political, axiological, and epistemological bases of the various arguments proposed in the field? The literature of peace studies is vast and covers many subtopics. Rather than discussing each area individually, I have identified a common thread of discussion appearing in the literature: an emphasis on democracy and democratization, which, no matter the ideological base, is seen as crucial. An examination of the literature uncovers three major ideologies: liberalism, liberationism, and transformationism. These three perspectives voice the dominant arguments in peace studies today. I will begin by examining why the field of peace studies views the basis of democracy as vital, followed by an in-depth exploration and critique of the positions of liberalism, liberationism, and transformationism.

Emphasis on Democracy; Democratization

The literature repeatedly stresses the importance of democratization and democratic teaching practices. Democracy, however defined, is seen as the necessary cornerstone of a just and peaceful society. "An informed public provides the basis of democracy.... The main task for Peace Education is to strengthen confidence in democracy and its capacity for solving problems" (Harris 1988, 21). Johan Galtung tells us: "Peace education, in short, is a question of practicing democracy in the most consequential... area: peace and war" (1988, 255). Therefore, preparing students to be good and informed participants in a democracy is of top concern. One key way of assuring democracy is not only to teach it, but to live it in the classroom.

Peace education empowers us for democracy. It teaches first hand about the democratic process, and prepares us to live effectively and responsibly in a democracy. Peace educator John Hurst says:

> Peace studies must be democratic in the true sense of the word. Peace studies students should be prepared to make critical decisions and tough analyses, leading to wise and informed judgments. The educational setting must be democratic itself if it is to teach students to live in a truly democratic way.... If the goals of Peace Studies, as well as education's historic purposes in democratic societies, are to be achieved—that is, the development of active citizens dedicated to democratic values and the public

good—the end of education cannot be the mere acquisition of knowledge. Rather, the end must be critically informed judgment and wise action. Knowledge alone does not either motivate or enable people to live democratically (1987, 84).

Certain conditions must be present in the classroom if it is to be truly democratic. It must be open for frank communication, yet remain critical. In other words, one should look as clearly as possible at an issue and understand it as thoroughly as possible in order to judge it carefully and skillfully. The classroom must be participatory and active, involving the student. The atmosphere must be one of equality, and the emphasis must be placed on the individual.

Critical, open discussions, so crucial to peace studies, mean at least to resist the temptation to present only one's own view. If peace studies is to be value-based, which it must be, then it has to remain critical of and open to all ideas. All sides of any issue should be brought out and discussed so that students are being *exposed* to views, not having various views *imposed* upon them (Scott 1987, 100). As Nigel Young says, "The co-operative search for truth is part of the participatory value of peace education. There is no claim of a monopoly of right" (Young 1987, 29).

A very strong emphasis on communication and fostering communication skills surfaces frequently in the literature. Two-way communication is especially important, keeping in mind that the teacher is sometimes student, and the student, also, teacher. Peter Dale Scott concludes that the peace educator must be committed to open, two-way communication, self-critical, objective (as opposed to neutral, in the sense of value-free), and democratic (1987, 100). A vital part of these critical, open discussions is that the students become active in them, and participate fully. Though well-honed communication abilities are important in almost all aspects of life, they are especially crucial in the area of conflict resolution and negotiation. Therefore, open, critical discussions will not only help the student become a better thinker and scholar, it will help to create better conflict mediators.

To be democratic, peace studies experiences must be participatory and varied. Students must be active learners. As Kent Shifferd, peace studies program director at Northland College tells us, "[S]tudents who learn to sit quietly as passive receivers of 'Truth' from an authority figure will have learned to function well in an authoritarian society" (1988, 186). Shifferd suggests that peace studies be problem-centered and co-intentional, meaning that the teacher and students co-direct their attention to a problem. He believes that the teacher and students should together "design and create a rigorous learning experience" to "directly and actively engage the students in problem-solving" (Shifferd 1988, 187). Democracy cannot be successful without full participation from its citizens (as exemplified by the ever-dwindling voter turn-out in the United States). Part of this conviction rests on "educating the whole child" in a Deweyan sense. Peace studies must not only engage the brain, it must speak to as many senses and aspects of the student as possible.

This participatory nature also must extend beyond the classroom walls. "It is important to recognize . . . that a conviction for and a commitment to constructing a just world peace cannot be taught, cannot be transferred by technique. It must be experienced by the learner in actual social contexts and action beyond the classroom" (Bryan 1989, 95). Therefore, it is widely agreed, though less widely practiced, that an internship or some co-curricular learning activity is crucial to the peace studies curriculum, thus labeling the field as "applied."

In order for the educational process to be democratic, the student and the teacher must be seen and treated as equals. Equal respect should be given to each alike. Though the teacher has certain faculties, abilities, and knowledge that the student does not, his/her authority should come from being considered an advanced student. The teacher is a guide and facilitator, not a purveyor of truth. Because of this equality, students are much more free in the classroom to guide their learning process than is now the case in most colleges. Again, the underlying theme is preparation for life in a democracy, always with the hope of improving on and creating better forms of democracy. Because the student is on equal footing with the teacher, the student has a greater responsibility in her or his education.

Individualized education also is central to peace education. The emphasis on teaching the individual that is prevalent in the writings also comes from the influence of John Dewey. Many peace studies scholars agree that gaining some level of personal inner peace is as important as working toward outward or societal peace. "One's capacity to achieve a degree of personal tranquillity and balance and calm is an essential prerequisite, I would suggest, to an ability to create a peaceful society . . . if one is able to create and preserve a peaceful personality, it does spread" (Kaye 1987, 1). After all, as Hicks reminds us, "Education for peace is initially about individual actors on the world stage" (1988, 248). If peace education is to succeed, it must be taught peacefully. There is no other way. This means that the peace educator also must be searching for this inner peace, a central tranquillity or ease from which to teach.

> Peace education rests on the assumption that the way to change social systems riddled by violence and committed to war is to change oneself. Until people change one by

> one they are not going to change by the thousands. . . .
> Peace educators can best become change agents by paying attention to the changes they themselves go through as they address the issues of war and peace and listening carefully to the concerns of others (Harris 1988, 158).

Although this is a difficult area to address, most peace scholars and teachers believe that the question of inward peace should not be neglected. As will be discussed, the transformationalists, in particular, find the area of personal peace to be essential to global peace.

Though early in the history of peace research, the role of conflict was disputed, it is now wholly agreed that conflict is a necessary and natural part of life. There are conflicts of interests, beliefs, points of view, theoretical conflicts and behavioral conflicts—all produced by the rich and vast diversity of life. Given the critical, open, democratic nature of peace education, it is natural that conflicts will arise in the classroom. Conflict, when controlled and nonviolent, often serves as a positive influence, creating a growth experience. Most authors agree that human beings will always have aggressive tendencies; though this does not condemn us to a life of war and violence. Kenneth Boulding believes that "conflict conducted in a decent and responsible manner is essential to any form of progress" (Wehr and Washburn 1976, 36). Peace studies is not out to eliminate all conflict; it simply wants to remove the violence from conflict, and conduct it in a "civilized" and productive manner. To summarize, the main thread running through the literature in the field is an emphasis on democracy and democratization, which consists of: critical, open communication; participatory and active education; emphasis on equality; emphasis on the individual; and conflict as necessary and natural. Next, I will examine the ideological bases found in the literature.

Three broad categories that represent the main ideologies in the literature are: liberalism, liberationism, and transformationism. I identify the political and epistemological assumptions underlying each of the three positions and trace the significant historical and philosophical trends in each. I discuss the main authors who built the theoretical foundations of these three approaches to peace studies. To set the framework for these three ideologies, I have created a chart comparing their philosophical, political, economic, and methodological foundations, along with other basic elements (see Figure 2.)

Liberalism

The vast majority of writings in the field of peace studies fall into the category of political and educational liberalism, particularly those that are British and American. The political liberal advocates "gradual, small-scale reforms within the framework of the existing political system in order to further individual freedom and to maximize the fullest realization of human potential" (O'Neill 1983, 183). Political liberals have faith in the government as a means of improving the human condition and believe in majority rule with minority rights. Liberals favor private ownership of the means of production, but do not support laissez faire capitalism. In the educational realm, the characteristic most highly valued is critical intelligence, which is defined in terms of "effective problem solving on both the personal and social levels" (O'Neill 1983, 184). The ultimate goal for the educational liberal is self-realization. The educational liberal looks to free the individual *within* the state and find equity *within* the system, rather than

Figure 2. The Three Representative Educational Ideologies in Peace Studies

	Liberalism	**Liberationism**	**Transformationism**
Ultimate Goal	Individual Self-Realization	Individual Self-Realization	Individual Self-Realization
Philosophical Foundations	Postivistic, "Old Paradigm," International Relations Model	Continental Tradition, Phenomenology Hermeneutics, Critical Theory	New Paradigm, Gandhian Nonviolence
Political Model	Change within the existing system	Reconstruction of the state (new more humane institutions)	Move Beyond Nation-State Model Community-Based Government
Economic Model	Capitalism	Marxism and Socialism	Post-Marxist and Beyond? (Hazel Hendersen?)
Framework	Individual within Nation-State Model	Nation-State/Individual Dichotomy Oppressors/Oppressed	Focus on Unity-Oneness of All Life Complexity and Inter-relatedness
Belief in	Scientific Method—Pragmatism, materially based	Scientific Method—Humanism, Secular, materially based (sometimes Religious)	Humanism, Mystic, spiritually based—Retains, but is not limited by, Scientific Method
Methodology for Change	Reform	Revolution (possibly violent)	Non-violent Revolution, Pacifism

—continued—

	Liberalism	**Liberationism**	**Transformationism**
Approach to Change	Gradual	Immediate	Present into the Future
Transformational Focus	Individual Changes Within Existing Social Structures	Society (Institutions) Changes, Then the Individual	Simultaneous Individual and Social Transformation
Focus of Peace Study	Negative peace (Positive peace) Individual, Problem-centered	Positive Peace (Negative peace) Structural Violence	Positive Peace (Negative Peace) New Forms of Nonviolent Action
Pedagogical Style	Dialogue	Discourse	Conversation

The categorizations of liberalism and liberationism are generally based on William F. O'Neill's 1983 work, and the category of transformationism is an adaptation of Betty Reardon's transformational approach.

striving for a new or more equitable system (O'Neill 1983, 185).

The liberal view of education espouses open communication, reform, gradualism, individualism, rational thought and the scientific method, and is problem-focused. The long-range goal of this approach is to "preserve and improve the existing social order" through education (O'Neill 1983, 12). Educational liberalism is essentially a psychological or personalistic approach. While learning occurs in a social matrix, it is always personal and psychological in nature. Although the social affects the psychological, and vice versa, the psychological (the subjective) remains fundamental, and is the ultimate basis of all experience (O'Neill 1983, 191). This belief results in the heavy focus on individualism in liberal education. Educational liberalism precludes revolution, anarchism, and quick solutions, and, like all broad ideologies, has a range of representative positions. On the more conservative end of the spectrum is the mild method liberalism, represented by the work of Maria Montessori. The more moderate educational liberalism can be found in the work of John Dewey, which is a structured or directive approach. And a more radical type of liberalism, which is generally non-directive, is represented by A.S. Neill (O'Neill 1983, 12). Interpretations of these various forms of educational liberalism are the dominant voices in peace studies today.

Educating for Peace, by the National Council of English Teachers, was published in 1940 and is an example of the conservative interpretation of the liberal nature of peace studies in its earliest stages. It deals with issues such as propaganda, the causes of war, and armaments as foreign policy. Peace education efforts focused on international relations in the curriculum and the study of war. They include two units on world peace, one of which includes as a suggested activity debating the resolve that a nation's best guarantee of peace is to be prepared at all times for war. Most of the activities in these peace units revolve around the study of war, the military, weaponry, and so on. The book is heavily based in international relations, and does not focus on the study of positive peace, indicative of current peace education efforts. "Good citizenship" is deemed as very important for this book (see the unit on International Good Will). The overwhelming emphasis is on war. In all, this work is an example of the conservative, positivistic, and low-key nature of peace education in its infancy.

Also representative of the conservative interpretation of the liberal philosophy found in early peace education is Maria Montessori. Drawing on the work of Froebel, Pestalozzi and Rousseau, Montessori developed a new philosophy of primary and preprimary instruction during the beginning of this century. Her method stresses a free environment in which the self-construction of the child can take place. It focuses on "extensive motor and sensory training, individual instruction, and the early development of writing and reading skills" (O'Neill 1983, 198). While Montessori does advocate changes in teaching and classroom processes and environment in accordance with new psychological findings, she is not critical of the established goals or traditional content of institutional learning.

Of particular interest is that as early as 1943, when no real peace studies or peace education literature had been written, Montessori was able to detect that if one is going to study peace, one must not only study negative peace. "What is generally meant by peace is the ceasing of war. But this concept, a purely negative one, is not the real concept of peace" (Montessori 1943, 4-5). Before the terms "negative" and "positive" peace were even coined, she had tapped into one of the most important questions in peace studies today. "True peace, on the contrary, suggests the triumph of justice and love among [humankind]; it reveals the existence of a better world wherein harmony reigns" (Montessori 1943, 7). She believes we can bring about peace through better education, making children better people and better citizens. "If we wish to set about a sane psychical rebuilding of [humankind], we must go back to the child. . . . We must turn to the child as a MESSIAH, an inspired being, a regenerator of our race and society" (Montessori 1943, 16). Montessori's hopes for peace boil down to improving human nature through better education.

Much of the theoretical foundations of liberal peace education were laid by John Dewey. Dewey, unquestionably the most important American educational philosopher, wrote voluminously; his career spanned many decades and his theories cannot be easily summarized. Dewey's early writings are the definitive basis of liberal peace education. In general, Dewey advocated objective inquiry, problem solving, and scientific verification. He called for education to be centered on the child's interests, social activities, and natural instincts, and for the teacher to have affection for and sympathy toward the child. Education, in his view, should be spontaneous, interactive, and allow for individual freedom and initiative. It should address not only the child's intellectual growth, but also her emotional, physical, cultural, psychological, social, and spiritual growth. He placed emphasis on the value of experience and preparation for social life. In all, he supported humane cultivation of critical intelligence. These qualities are the basic characteristics valued by liberal peace educators.

Four representatives of the liberal position in peace studies today are Kenneth Boulding, Fisher and Ury, and Jean Bethke Elshtain. As peace studies slowly began to grow in the mid to late 1950s, efforts in the development of peace research in the United States and Britain increasingly focused on the scientific method. The ultimate development in the liberal emphasis on scientific method is represented in peace studies by Kenneth Boulding, an American economist. Boulding, with his wife Elise, started the second peace studies program in the U.S. at the University of Michigan in 1955. Boulding was highly aware of the ambiguous nature of studying peace; therefore, to avoid ambiguity, the program centered specifically on conflict resolution and he did not use the word "peace" in the title of the program. He was determined that peace studies be a manageable, concrete, measurable topic, using scientific, empirical methods, and yielding verifiable results. The fruit of this process came as a landmark book by Boulding in 1978 called *Stable Peace*.

Many peace researchers and scholars consider this short book to be one of the most important works on peace and peace policy. Boulding uses negative peace (absence of physical violence) as his conceptual framework exclusively throughout the book. For example, in this book, cold war qualifies as peace. Boulding actually defines peace and war using a diagram (1978, 43). He charts strain on the Y axis, and strength on the X axis. With a 45 degree line moving upward, he charts where war and peace lie on this grid; what he is ostensibly doing is measuring peace. His point is that we need to increase strength and diminish strain. Though Boulding notes the complexity of war and peace— "War and peace are part of the vast Shiva's dance of the universe in which everything has multiple causes and multiple effects, in which the attempt to identify the sole cause of anything is doomed to frustration" (47)—in his attempt to make peace into manageable, legitimate, scientific subject matter, he denies that very complexity.

The conflict resolution approach to peace studies also represents the liberal position on peace education. The landmark work in the field of conflict resolution came in 1983 as a result of the Harvard Negotiation Project. Written by Roger Fisher and William Ury, *Getting to Yes* takes a rational, problem-oriented look at conflict resolution and management. The authors draw out the problems with negotiating, the methods used, and the possibility of unforeseen complications. They argue that any negotiation may be judged by three criteria: "It should produce a wise agreement if agreement is possible. It should be efficient. And it should improve or at least not damage the relationship" (Fisher and Ury 1983, 4). Positional bargaining, or arguing from a pre-set position, is the most common problem with successful conflict resolution. The authors argue that such bargaining produces unwise agreements, is inefficient, and often harms relationships. Positionally, people choose to be either soft or hard bargainers, which doesn't work. The entire method needs to be changed. The new method that the authors have developed is called *principled negotiation* or *negotiation on the merits* (Fisher and Ury 1983, 11). This method has four main points: separate the people from the problem; focus on interests, not positions; generate a variety of possibilities before deciding what to do; and insist that the result be based on some objective standard (Fisher and Ury 1983, 11). This method humanizes the process of conflict negotiation in many ways. People use imagination and create new options. The ultimate goal is mutual gain for both parties. Conflict resolution is reformed, humanized, and civilized through the use of critical intelligence.

Nuclear studies or nuclear education, the other major branch found in peace studies, also falls squarely in the liberal perspective.

Jean Bethke Elshtain, also representative of the politically liberal position, examines the many roles played by men and women during wartime. She explores the history of "armed civic virtue," and follows the long discourse on war and politics from Plato to Machiavelli to Marx and Hegel, and beyond. Elshtain tells us that while everyone says they support peace, we are all actually caught up in a great, master narrative: the war narrative. War makes us feel ALIVE. As one woman put it: "You know that I do not love war or want it to return. But at least it made me feel alive, as I have not felt alive before or since" (Elshtain 1987, 10). War provides an incredible challenge, the pushing to physical and psychological limits, the drawing together of community. Elshtain raises many questions: How can we get beyond the master war narrative? Is there, or can we create, a master peace narrative? While she does not attempt to answer these questions directly, she does make it clear that she supports the concept of the nation-state and believes in the liberal, democratic model of government. This work exemplifies the problem-centered liberal approach. If we want to eradicate war, we must first study and understand it. In all, Elshtain's rational and analytic description of war and gender roles in war is an extremely important contribution to peace studies.

Looking at the representatives of the liberal spectrum of peace studies as a whole, we find certain common values and beliefs. The liberal view of education seeks to reform education gradually from the inside out, with the goal of preserving and improving upon the current social order through better education (O'Neill 1983, 12). It seeks change within the system rather than transformation or replacement of the system. The liberal view embraces rational thought and the scientific method and focuses on objective inquiry and verifiability. It emphasizes problem solving at the personal and social levels and values the development of critical intelligence. In the classroom, the liberal view caters to the individual. It is humanistic and supports individual freedom, initiative, spontaneity, and subsequent responsibility. It emphasizes open communication and interactive experience, with the ultimate goal being individual self-realization.

Overall, representatives of the liberal view of peace education support the nation-state model and have faith in liberal, democratic government. (The nation-state model of government is generally comprised of sovereign political bodies, occupying and defending a particular geographic area.) Liberals work for peace through gradual reforms within the system with the belief that better education can truly make a better world. Educational liberalism "seeks to alter existing educational practices and policies without, at the same time, seeking to modify existing social institutions in any significant sense in the process" (O'Neill 1983, 196). This is the main difference between the educational liberals and the liberationists: educational liberalism does not support revolution or a new social order, while educational liberationism deems these as necessary for the creation of peace.

Liberationism

Liberationists maintain that "we should seek the immediate large-scale reform of the established political order as a way of furthering individual liberties and promoting the maximum realization of personal potential" (O'Neill 1983, 12). In order for individuals to reach personal happiness and self-realization, development of new and more humanistic social institutions is required (O'Neill 1983, 8). Liberationists call for rapid and sweeping changes in the basic nature of the existing social order. The ultimate goal in educational liberationism is "to implement the reconstruction of society along truly humanistic lines that emphasize the fullest development of each person's unique potentialities as a human being" (O'Neill 1983, 311). The vast majority of educational liberationists, unlike the liberals, believe that

> [T]he social necessarily takes precedence over the individual. . . . The distinction between the social and the psychological is essentially spurious. Personal experience is always experienced in and through some particular cultural framework. The learner is essentially and necessarily social, and [s/he] always operates by and through a "socialized psyche"—based on a particular set of cultural constraints that govern the nature of virtually all personal experience. Civilized man [sic] is essentially a social phenomenon . . . the individual is always a particular expression of the social. Whether "individualism" will exist, and how much "individualism" will be expressed, is invariably determined by the nature and dynamics of some particular culture at some particular point in time (O'Neill 1983, 311).

Educational liberationism ranges from reform (e.g. Civil and Women's Rights Movements) to radical (e.g. George Counts, Theodore Brameld) to revolutionary (e.g. Marxist, Paulo Freire) (O'Neill 1983, 13).

While liberalism generally represents the early phase of peace studies, liberationism in the United States was born of the events of the 1960s: the Cuban missile crisis, the Partial Test Ban Treaty, the Vietnam War, the invasion of Czechoslovakia. New questions were raised and "critical peace research" was born. Peace researchers began to ask "What are the mechanisms of dominance and exploitation between and within nations? What are the objective, even if latent, conflicts defined by them? How can these conflicts be made manifest so as to make it possible to resolve them? How can liberation be achieved? Can peace researchers avoid taking sides in these conflicts, and what is their proper role" (Wiberg 1988, 45)? Out of this era came the integration into peace research of "the Marxist research tradition on imperialism, the Latin American dependencia school, and the emerging 'peace education' movement" (Wiberg 1988, 45).

In the forefront of raising these critical questions on structural violence was peace researcher Johan Galtung. Galtung, by far the most prolific and influential scholar in the field of peace studies, is founder and former director of the International Peace Research Institute (IPRA) in Oslo, Norway. I am placing Galtung in the liberationist camp because of his emphasis on positive peace and structural violence. Though not easily categorized, he is the most important peace researcher to date. The history of the development of the main ideas in peace research over the last twenty-five years could easily be a Galtung biography. As discussed in Chapter 1, two of the most important contributions to peace studies, the negative/positive peace distinction and the construct of structural violence, were contributed by Johan Galtung. Galtung views peace research as an effort to explore the conditions of peace in a holistic and global manner (1988, 248). He sees the basic concern of peace research as the reduction of all types of violence. Galtung identifies the ten major dilemmas of peace research conducted over the last 25 years as:

> [T]he definition of peace research; peace as absence of violence (including structural violence); violence as obstacles to basic needs satisfaction; extension to peace in nature, human and social spaces (not only the global space); the dialectic between research, education and action; the social role of the peace researcher; the basic strategies of peace action; the methods of peace research;

the choice of intellectual style; and the conception of peace in various civilizations (1985, 141).

Galtung is quick to note, "The problem is how to weave values in general, and the broad family of values referred to as 'peace' in particular, into the paradigm of intellectual activity, not as a detachable prologue or epilogue, but as an indelible part of intellectual activity itself" (1988, 244). Galtung concludes that highest priority should be given to critical predictions, theory formation, and positive constructions, and on peace education and action guided by these explorations (1988, 257).

Most scholars categorize three liberationist positions in peace studies: feminist, Marxist and critical theory. For purposes of this review, I categorize the positions specifically according to the literature of peace studies. In general, feminist positions in peace studies take a reformist position, although some begin to move toward the radical. The Marxist and socialist positions are more radical to revolutionary, and critical theory lies at the revolutionary end of the liberationist spectrum. The liberationists are more heavily influenced by the "continental philosophers" and the "grand theory" traditions, such as phenomenology and hermeneutics, than by the positivistic methods of Western science.

Most of the feminist positions in peace studies represent liberationism. Barbara Roberts exemplifies this position, arguing that peace research has generally taken a male perspective to the exclusion of women as a visible social category (1984, 195). This pattern has led to several problems for peace research. Since "the most common form of direct physical violence in our society appears to be men against women . . . the most severe consequences of indirect structural violence are suffered by women . . . [and] gender is among the most fundamental determinants of inequality in the world," peace research must examine the patterns of violence against women and the gender relationships of power and powerlessness if it is to be meaningful (Roberts 1984, 195).

Birgit Brock-Utne is the foremost scholar on feminism in relation to peace and peace education. According to Brock-Utne, the radical and socialist feminist arguments are:

> [M]aking the radical feminist distinction between *power-over* [power as dominance] and *power-to* [power as competence] a central distinction . . . incorporating an analysis of patriarchy and an insistence on seeing private and personal experiences as political . . . not only realizing the fundamental oppression of women everywhere but that this oppression varies according to class, race, and culture. Not all women are more oppressed than all men. But generally, women are more oppressed than men of their own race, caste, or class (1989, 73).

Brock-Utne examines socialization into violence and aggression, the learning of obedience, loyalty, and competitiveness, and suggests that for formal education to be made more conducive to the learning and creation of peace, certain changes must take place. For instance, history books should be rewritten to include the history of nonviolence and the lives of women; the teaching of constructive thinking and conflict management must be part of the normal curriculum; classroom focus should be shifted to cooperation, sharing, and joy, rather than competition; and grading should be kept to a minimum (Brock-Utne 1989, 173-74). Ultimately, Brock-Utne's vision is that an infusion of feminism and peace perspectives into the formal and informal educational sectors will have the power to criticize and reconstruct our socioeconomic institutions leading to a more equitable and humane culture.

Marxist and socialist perspectives on peace education, however defined, span the radical and revolutionary approaches to educational liberationism, in which replacing the capitalist system with a more humane economic system, such as socialism, is a priority. "While [Marx] holds to the logical and psychological primacy of society over the individual descriptively, [he] calls for the reconstruction of society for the ultimate purpose of correcting this situation" (O'Neill 1983, 17). Peace studies and Marxism both have as an ultimate goal a vision of qualitative social change leading to a world of peace, freedom, justice, and equality.

Peter Dale Scott (not himself a Marxist) argues that if peace studies, much of which now belittles or ignores Marxism, is to speak with the second or third world at all, it must take seriously the theories of Marxism. For him, the great strength of Marxism is "to see that material forces underlie social systems, through dialectic interactions which . . . force humans to 'make their own history, but . . . not . . . just as they please'," while its weakness is to "dehumanize its own vision, to the point where history is no longer a matter of people at all, but only of classes or economic conditions" (Scott 1983, 352). In Marxism, the transformation of the state is paramount:

> In its preoccupation with external political power, in its separatist appeal to the dictatorship of either an industrialized or a peasant proletariat, in its postponement of needed personal changes until after the revolution, it has never been able to achieve the goal of a classless society which is one of its most attractive features . . . (Scott 1983, 361-62).

Marxism does not explain the power of nonviolent movements, nor does it address mysticism, aesthetics, or the fact that technology and production have not brought about happiness for most people. Yet, Marxism does provide critical analyses which peace studies should address. Scott stresses that peace studies and Marxism can learn a tremendous amount from each other's strengths and weaknesses.

Although Marxism does not explain everything, it remains a potent theory. An attempt to harness that potency and correct and account for Marxism's weaknesses is found in critical theory, which represents the revolutionary approach to educational liberationism. Revolutionary educational liberationism argues that

> since the schools are institutions that serve the larger interests of the general culture, and, since the culture itself is the major educational force in the life of the child, the schools themselves cannot realistically hope to reconstruct the society by any sort of internal criticism of existing practices; [rather, they must work for] the active abolition of the existing system and for its replacement by a different kind of society founded upon truly humane and rational principles (O'Neill 1983, 313).

Critical theory comes out of the work of the Frankfurt School of social theory, associated with the Institute of Social Research in Frankfurt, founded in the late 1920s. The major theorists associated with the Frankfurt School are Max Horkheimer, Theodor Adorno, Herbert Marcuse, and Jurgen Habermas (Giddens 1985, 123).

> Though members of the Frankfurt School were Marxists ... they were very far from being Marxists of an orthodox persuasion. They regarded Marxism as a flexible, critical approach to the study of society, not as a fixed and inviolable set of doctrines. They were prepared to jettison ideas that to most other Marxists are essential to what Marxism is as a body of thought and a guide to political practice. Thus, they held, for example, that the working class has become integrated into capitalist society, and is no longer a revolutionary force.... The Frankfurt School argued that capitalism has changed so much since Marx's

time that many of Marx's concepts have to be discarded or at least radically altered (Giddens 1985, 123). The Frankfurt school opened up a reworking or an extension of the classical Marxist question of base and superstructure through Althusser's structural Marxism, Gramsci's writings on hegemony, Levi-Strauss' structural linguistics, and Chang's proposed discourse analysis to account for power that appears independent of base and superstructure (Steeves 1987, 110).

Critical theory rebels against the positivism and determinism of classical Marxism, with its "iron laws" of forces of production, operating mechanically to influence social change (Giddens 1985, 123). It strives to reunite theory and practice, which Marx failed to do. Marx was wrong to believe that social forces are immutable, like laws of nature (Giddens 1985, 126). He left no room for active interaction of human beings in their own fate. If human behavior is governed by ineluctable laws and there is nothing we can do to shape our own history by actively intervening in it, what is the point of being a Marxist (Giddens 1985, 125)? Habermas radically defends human freedom, arguing that humans are self-reflective; they can reflect on their history and change it. Critical theory is concerned with "achieving rational autonomy of action, free from domination . . . critical theory must recognize that an emancipated society would be one in which human beings actively control their own destinies, through a heightened understanding of the circumstances in which they live" (Giddens 1985, 127).

Peace researcher Hayward Alker believes that emancipatory knowledge interest, in a Habermasian sense, distinguishes peace research. It "forms a most important basis for the disciplinary distinctiveness of peace research" (1988, 220). Habermas describes emancipatory knowledge interest as "an attitude which is formed in the experience of suffering from something man-made [sic], which can be abolished and should be abolished" (Alker 1988, 220). Alker believes we need a major change in scientific thinking to escape the "defeatist, flat, empiricist, naturally exploitive conception of reality that underlies too much of contemporary behavioral science and empirical peace research" (1988, 236-7). How does peace research qualify for emancipatory knowledge interest? First by demonstrating that war is human-made, second by arguing that war should be abolished, and third by trying to establish that it can be ended.

Marguerite Rivage-Seul argues that pedagogy for peace has been ineffective because it rests on "technical reason," a positivist view of knowledge valuing objective, scientific standards. In order for peace education to become effective, it must engage the imagination in a moral fashion to get beyond the impersonal stance of typical peace pedagogy. Rivage-Seul develops a view of moral imagination based on the ideas of Paulo Freire and Franz Hinkelammert, whose theories are strikingly similar. According to both, "moral imagination means envisioning possibilities for human welfare from the standpoint of the world's poor, who alone are capable of liberating the non-poor from the latter's socially-defined perceptual limits of possibility" (Rivage-Seul 1987, 55). This view encompasses the intersubjectivity of life, the necessity of practical action, and "implies recognizing, understanding, and adopting a critical viewpoint on the nuclear arms race" (Rivage-Seul 1987, 169). It opens the curricula of peace education to what the poor have to teach. In all, Rivage-Seul's moral imagination takes a wholly other than American/European perspective. If peace education is ever going to be effective, it must not only get beyond the positivistic paradigm, it must assume a truly global perspective. This method of moral imagination accomplishes both.

Arguably the most important critical theorist in the area of education is Paulo Freire. Freire, a Brazilian, was a professor of education before being banned from his country for his radical work and ideas. Freire combines his beliefs in Catholicism, Marxist Humanism, and practical educational and political involvement (Matthews 1980, 88). He sees pedagogy as empowerment for critical action and has worked extensively with literacy problems. For Freire, "Knowledge is derived from experience and is gained and tested in practice, in the active engagement of human subjects in the transformation of the natural and social world" (Matthews 1980, 89). "Praxis" (unity of thought and action,) empowerment, liberation, and "conscientization," are key terms in the Freirian approach. "Conscientization" (*conscientizaçao*) "refers to learning to perceive social, political, and economic contradictions, and to take action against the oppressive elements of reality" (Freire 1970, 19). Matthews writes that "features of [Freire's epistemological] landscape are: realism, subjectivism, abstraction, codification, distancing, agency, problematizing, causality, holism, fallibilism, and a social dimension" (1980, 97). Two now famous ideas Freire brought us in *Pedagogy of the Oppressed* are the "banking" concept of education (information being deposited or fed to the student for future withdrawal) as oppressive, and "dialogics" as an instrument of liberation.

In summary, liberationism calls for immediate, large-scale reform of oppressive and exploitative institutions to reconstruct the state in a more humanistic fashion. It generally supports revolution, including potentially violent revolution. Societal change takes precedence over individual change. Educational liberationism in peace studies is grounded in the philosophies of feminism, Marxism and socialism, and critical theory, which are in turn, grounded in the continental traditions of phenomenology and hermeneutics. Educationally, liberationists are more radical than the liberals. They focus on issues of structural violence and empowerment, addressing the concerns of positive peace more often than the liberals. The various forms of educational liberationism found in peace studies focus on positive peace and structural violence. Main topics of concern include relationships of power and dominance, structures of oppression and exploitation, methods of liberation, and radical and revolutionary transformation of our socio-economic institutions, particularly patriarchy and capitalism.

Transformationism

Unlike liberalism and liberationism, transformationism is a relatively new approach (developed over the last forty years) that has yet to prove its efficacy. The transformationists represent a variety of approaches, all of which center on the individual and individual action, and move beyond the confines of the nation-state model to consider new and innovative community and political relationships. Transformationists are action-oriented and step out of the boundaries of the theories discussed previously. They are not talking about the same premises, or asking the same questions. In contrast to the gradualist reform of liberalism or the organized revolution or immediate, radical reform of liberationism, transformationists seem to focus on individuals living and acting moment to moment. Although groups and organizations are viewed as important and influential, power for change is seen as resting in the hands of each individual. In other words, individuals are not powerless without a group or organization. Unlike the liberationists, transformationists do not believe that socioeconomic institutions have to be reformed or replaced before meaningful action can take place. Transformationism jettisons the left-right dichotomy; the transformationist vein of peace studies has been developing for roughly twenty years.

The transformationist approach espouses nothing less than profound cultural change. Transformation of consciousness is primary, though behavioral and structural changes also play a role. The fundamental causes of war, violence, and oppression lie in the way we think. Transformationists believe we must have fundamental changes in our values and modes of thinking if we are to find lasting peace. Heavy emphasis lies on the creation of new knowledge and the value of creative imagination. Teachers use many methods, with the tendency being toward praxis and holistic learning. The two foundational ideas in the transformationist approach, which distinguish it from liberalism and liberationism, are an emphasis on the strategy of nonviolence (as philosophy, revolution, and action) and a focus on the new paradigm.

Nonviolence

That nonviolence underlies all efforts for peace is an essential premise of the transformationist perspective. The most important figure in the history of modern nonviolent struggle is undoubtedly Gandhi. For Gandhi, nonviolence is more natural than violence. It is rooted in humankind's "natural disposition to love" (Merton 1965, 43). In Gandhi's method of nonviolent change,

> the process of reform in the individual did not await final transformation in the society. . . . A truly liberated indi-

> vidual was to him the most effective instrument of social transformation.... Both in the forms of struggle as well as in the tasks of social reconstruction Gandhi gave little importance to the State. So his methodology was not based on the capture or destruction of [the] State. He wanted the local initiative at the grass-roots level to play the dominant role in struggle and reconstruction (Dandavate 1977, 49).

Gandhi was concerned with the individual, not the state. "In Gandhi's and King's fusion of the personal and the political, one strives to create now, in oneself and in one's movement, the processes of interaction one desires for the future" (Scott 1983, 360). In his conception of nonviolence and creating a peaceful future, Gandhi saw no room for discrepancy between means and ends. Thich Nhat Hanh, Vietnamese peace activist and Zen scholar, argues that to create peace, we must first ourselves be peace: "Every day we do things, we are things, that have to do with peace. If we are aware of our lifestyle, our way of consuming, of looking at things, we will know how to make peace right in the moment we are alive" (1987, 65-66). Hanh concludes: "Without being peace, we cannot do anything for peace.... It we are not peaceful, then we cannot contribute to the peace movement.... Peace work means, first of all, being peace" (1987, 80). In the end, the responsibility of being peace rests with each one of us. Transformationists build on this philosophy of personal nonviolence to develop nonviolent group strategies and action.

In the transformationist view of peace studies, one of the most important concepts or strategies is nonviolent revolution, developed substantially through the work of Gene Sharp and George Lakey. The basis of nonviolent revolution is "the belief that the exercise of power depends on the consent of the ruled who, by withdrawing that consent, can control and even destroy the power of their opponent" (Sharp 1973, 4). As Merton pointed out, the only successful way of abolishing an institution is to uncover what its basic functions are and find alternative ways in which they can be fulfilled (Lakey 1987, 9). Lakey argues that the four major institutions responsible for the world's misery are: militarism, monopoly capitalism, nationalism, and violence, all of which feed off of and survive on each other. For Lakey, the four things that can counteract these are: civilian-based defense, socialism, world government, and nonviolent struggle (1987, 194). Sharp believes that although nonviolent techniques are extremely powerful, they remain a largely neglected and underdeveloped political technique (1973, 808).

How do the transformationist's view of nonviolence, being peace, nonviolent revolution, simultaneous self and societal transformation, and transcendence of the nation-state model translate into practice? Are there any specific instances we can turn to as examples of these processes in action? The women's peace encampment at Greenham Common, a U.S. missile base located on the outskirts of Newbury, England exemplifies the major characteristics of the transformationist approach.

The U.S. Air Force planned to deploy ninety-six ground-launched, mobile cruise missiles to the base by 1983. To protest this new build-up in the arms race, thirty-six women of varying backgrounds set out on a nine-day walk to the camp in the summer of 1981. The press ignored their walk and their cause, so, when they arrived, four women chained themselves to the main gate. Days and then weeks went by before the country, and then the world, took note. Though the original marchers had no intention of staying at Greenham, their protest turned into a permanent encampment, denouncing the weapons, the military, and the arms race. They erected make-shift tents and communication systems. What began as a walk turned into a very powerful movement. The great joy of Greenham is its innovation, imagination, and freedom. None of the rules of society, culture, or institutions hold sway. "These women are disobedient, disloyal to civilization, experienced in taking direct action, advanced in their ability to make a wide range of political connections" (Snitow 1985, 44). The women are leaderless—there are no ringleaders to arrest. Many forms of communication are used, but small affinity groups linked through a larger network predominate. Decisions are made by individuals, small groups, and at times, large groups; discussion can last minutes or days. The Greenham women are "experimenting with self-governance in small communities; they are living with less, seeking new definitions of comfort and satisfaction" (Snitow 1985, 39).

A broader, more general example of transformationism can be found in the Green Movement, that values putting ecological wisdom, nonviolence, and grassroots democracy, among other things, into practice. The Green Movement hopes to decentralize and humanize socio-political-economic systems internationally. Greens support nationalized health care, worker and cooperatively owned businesses, and elimination of patriarchal practices. "In the United States, Greens have delineated ten key values of the movement: ecological wisdom, grassroots democracy, personal and social responsibility, nonviolence, decentralization, community-based economics, post-patriarchal values, respect for diversity (including religious pluralism), global responsibility, and future focus" (Spretnak 1988, 200). There are Green Parties across the globe, from Australia to Germany to Mexico. Although the Green Party has not yet had significant political impact outside Europe, general interest seems to be growing. Green Movement organizations and Green Parties are sprouting up in more countries; they may be able to provide a transformationist political vision of the future to work toward.

Paradigm Shift

Transformationism may be seen as indicative of a significant paradigm shift. In "Peace as a Paradigm Shift," Michael Nagler addresses paradigms in the Kuhnian sense. A paradigm is a recognized and accepted model, pattern, or worldview whose theoretical and methodological beliefs permit systematic evaluation and criticism. Nagler argues that the prevailing paradigm of war and militarism is reaching a crucial breaking point. Yet, what is needed to produce this break is not the shift spoken of by many social scientists, but a much deeper change of the kind referred to by Kuhn. It would take "a permanent shift in how we view the world; how we gauge hostility, what we think of to do about it—almost a shift in what we perceive as real" (Nagler 1981, 50). This shift would be exceedingly rare, for it would change not only our thinking about war, but also our relationships with one another. Is the time ripe for such a change? And how could people concerned with peace facilitate it?

Though not yet widely accepted, getting away from, evolving beyond, the "old paradigm" is a visible trend in peace studies. The old paradigm is connected to the positivistic approach based on the work of Newton and Descartes, hence the Newtonian-Cartesian paradigm. The positivistic approach is linear, deterministic, materialistic, and reductionistic and emphasizes prediction and control. It uses empirical methods of inquiry, the inductive and deductive methods and focuses on analytic rationality. Its model tends to be mechanistic, and tends to compartmentalize, fragment, and isolate things in order to study them.

> Peace research began in the rationalistic mode of international relations, and that was part of the problem. Peace researchers were belaboring to gather immense amounts of data on this or that military situation, rather than trusting many of their intuitions and searching for a more holistic examination of peace. The development of more fundamental ideas or theories on peace, or the attempt to influence or create new imagings of the world were seen as unscientific. . . . Positivism has been strongly criticized [by peace researchers], the positivistic, behavioral and quantitative approach to testing theories has been required to be complemented or altogether replaced by more holistic approaches, such as the hermeneutic philosophy of science (Harle 1987, 12).

What the new paradigm is moving away from is fragmentation, dualism, and rejection of subjective experience, among other things. Many scholars believe that peace studies cannot afford to remain within the confines of the waning paradigm. This is not a shocking realization—many traditional disciplines, such as physics, biology, and psychology, have come to the same conclusion. Carson and Gideonse state this need succinctly: "[P]eace education has the obligation to insist that human reason is a unity of logic, emotion, value, and will and that examinations of human reason must preserve its comprehensiveness and internal dignity" (1987, 9). It involves a redefinition of human reason.

Kenneth Boulding, in his landmark book, *Stable Peace*, states that "War is no longer legitimate, but peace is not yet legitimate." The key to taking delegitimization to its logical end is to find increasingly more effective means of peaceful conflict resolution so that we have a real and legitimate means of solving disputes (Nagler 1981, 52). One might say that the most agreed upon purpose of peace studies is the delegitimizing of war, leading to its eventual abolition. If war is becoming increasingly delegitimized, then we may be at the point of paradigm breakdown, but not yet of paradigm shift. There are growing anomalies, puzzles, things that simply don't fit into the old paradigm. But most people still buy into the old paradigm, and until a more significant number is convinced of its obsolescence, it will not collapse. In order for this to happen, the new paradigm must be made to be seen as a viable alternative.

Nagler argues that any successful use of nonviolence provides clear indication of a new paradigm, since it is based on an entirely different set of assumptions and relationships. Therefore, if we want to help bring about this paradigm shift, we should learn the history of nonviolence, understand the theory behind it, and—most importantly—learn to practice it. And wherever possible, we must show that cooperation and aid may be stronger than belligerency (Nagler 1981, 51). This is the basis of the transformationist peace effort. Nagler believes that without a shift in our educational perspectives, the transformation to a new paradigm will not take place.

By far the leading peace studies scholar in the transformationist approach is educator Betty Reardon. She conveys the primary goals of the transformationisst approach as: "(1) awareness of the significance of consciousness and culture to problems of structure and policy, and (2) the development of capacities to bring about social and cultural change" (Reardon 1989, 24). One reason the transformationist approach is so powerful is that it shifts "emphasis from instructing—imparting particular knowledge—to educating, which includes both the learning that educators elicit from students and the learning that educators themselves experience in that process" (Reardon 1988, 47). Reardon has created a fresh term for this perspective—"edu-learner"—which she describes as "a practitioner/theorist whose primary activity is learning while trying to help other people learn" (1988, 47). Reardon targets seven fundamental capacities of peace education: reflection, responsibility, risk, reconciliation, recovery, reconstruction, and reverence. In her view, these are the seven main qualities transformationist peace education needs to engage if it is to succeed. These seven capacities need to be developed and nurtured through four essential dimensions of comprehensive peace education: (1) integrated, holistic education in which the whole person, in the context of the whole planetary order, is at the center of the educational process, (2) the human context, (3) the ecological and the planetary, and (4) the organic and the developmental (Reardon 1988, 74-75). For Reardon, "Stated most succinctly, the general purpose of peace education . . . is to promote the development of an authentic planetary consciousness that will enable us to function as global citizens and to transform the present human condition by changing the social structures and the patterns of thought that have created it" (1988, x). She defines comprehensive peace education as "peace education that takes place at every level, and in every subject area, of formal education" (Reardon 1988, xii). Overall, Reardon's work is a clear voice for transformationist peace education.

The capacity of imaging a new future is an important part of the transformationist approach. Elise Boulding is a specialist in the areas of imaging and futurism, and believes we need to change or correct the image we have of our own peacemaking capacities. Boulding believes that we have a cultural glorification of violence, magnified by journalism and the media. Our cultural mirror is reflecting back a very unreal and distorted picture of our everyday lives. Peace learning must look with a critical eye at these distorted cultural images

(Boulding 1987, 6). One important and powerful way to combat this threat to peace is through imaging a peaceful world, which she sees as crucial to peace learning. Guided imagings of a peaceful world help to make the possibilities for such a state more real. Being able to imagine peaceful world situations is seen as critical to the capacity for humanity to create such a future. Ultimately, Boulding concludes that certain things are needed for peace learning: cognitive readiness, experiential learning, overcoming misleading cultural feedback, releasing intuition and imagination, and strong community support systems (1987, 10).

The transformationist approach aims at profound cultural change primarily through a transformation of consciousness. Because the fundamental causes of war, violence, and oppression lie in the way we think, basic changes in our values and modes of thinking are essential to creating a lasting peace. Formal transformationist pedagogy stresses praxis, holistic learning, and creation of new knowledge. It focuses on open conversation between equals, in which the instructor is considered as an "edu-learner" in the sense Reardon described. Transformationists value creative imagination and stress visualization. Transformationists do not concern themselves with the nation-state model or the liberal-conservative debate. Individual transformation does not wait for the transformation of socio-economic institutions or solidification of a more humane culture. Nonviolent strategy and action lie at the base of the transformationist perspective, and are seen as the main hope for the future. The transformationist approach is young and yet to be fully tested; still, if its epistemological and political basis and methods do prove successful, it might be the crucial blow to the old paradigm, pushing paradigm breakdown over the edge to paradigm shift, and thus providing the impetus necessary for acceptance of a new paradigm.

Summary

A review of the literature of peace studies reveals a strong emphasis on democracy and bringing democracy into the classroom. Democratization focuses on critical, open communication, active participation, freedom and equality, the individual as peacemaker, and nonviolent conflict as necessary, natural, and welcome. The three main ideologies found in peace studies are liberalism, liberationism, and transformationism. I examined the undergirdings, premises, and most influential scholars of each of these three belief systems. The boundaries of liberalism, liberationism, and transformationism drawn for purposes of categorization are abstract and to an extent, artificial. Liberals often agree with liberationists, transformationists agree with liberals, and so on. Overlap regularly occurs.

All three ideologies share certain beliefs, such as "the pursuit of knowledge through rational and scientific methods of problem-solving processes to the resolution of personal and social problems" (O'Neill 1983, 187). Each approach also stresses open communication. Reardon finds commonalities in instruction and teaching: All three approaches share value clarification and analysis and participatory modes of learning (Reardon 1989, 25). Each emphasizes the role of the individual, though in different ways. Liberalism honors the individual as the center of the educational practice and attempts to cater to her or him. Liberationism seeks to liberate each person through education, with the goal of uniting people in a revolution. Transformationism focuses on individual action and the power of the individual. All positions "prescribe individual experience and judgment—personal problem-solving ability, individual commitment to social liberation, or total and unrestrained self-determination—as taking precedence over all of the more traditional forms of authority and control" (O'Neill 1983, 17). All three ideologies exalt the individual in some form, the reason being that the ultimate goal for each approach is individual self-realization.

Liberalism focuses on gradual reform within the existing social and political system. It generally supports capitalism and the nation-state model of government. Educationally, it stresses rational, problem-centered, individualized learning, grounded in the scientific method. In peace studies, liberalism often clings to positivistic methods of analysis, thus limiting study to negative peace issues. Liberalism remains the historical and dominant voice in peace studies.

Liberationists view much of liberalism as harmful in the sense that its reorganizing of old educational objectives and content in new and more efficient ways actually serves to strengthen conservatism in education and perpetuate the status quo (O'Neill 1983, 19). "Without a collective commitment to individual self-actualization as an overall social ideal, the attempt to promulgate 'individualism' as an educational objective is merely a rhetorical device to distract attention from underlying social authoritarianism" (O'Neill 1983, 312). The liberationist sees the main mistake of liberalism as giving the personal (the individual) priority over the social (including the political). Liberationists argue that individual critical thinking "is impossible in the absence of a political system that encourages and sustains the social and intellectual conditions that are prerequisites for a fully developed popular intelligence" (O'Neill 1983, 187).

Liberationists call for immediate, large-scale reform or replacement of oppressive and exploitative institutions to reconstruct the state in a more humanistic fashion. Liberationism generally supports revolution, including potentially violent revolution. Societal change takes precedence over individual change. Educational liberationism in peace studies draws from the philosophies of feminism, Marxism and socialism, and critical theory, which are in turn, grounded in the continental traditions of phenomenology and hermeneutics. Educationally, liberationists are more radical than the liberals, focusing on issues of structural violence and empowerment, and addressing the concerns of positive peace more often than the liberals.

Liberationism is not without its own problems. "In a similar sense, it can be argued that the . . . liberationist does not 'liberate' at all but merely reinforces the existing system by correcting some of its more blatant abuses, abuses that, if allowed to run their course, might eventuate in a demand for truly radical changes within the overall system" (O'Neill 1983, 19). Though the liberationist perspective provides a powerful critique, it excludes from the outset possibilities such as aesthetics and mysticism. Like the liberal perspective, it remains tied to a material critique, which limits it by emphasizing reductionistic causality. One of the crucial flaws of both liberalism and liberationism is that both fail to move beyond the nation-state model, which consequently stifles their envisioning of alternative peaceful worlds. Capitalism, generally espoused by the liberals, tends to result in war; Marxism, generally espoused in some form by the liberationists, has until recently produced murderous revolutions. "Ultimately both perspectives, though for different reasons, tend to belittle movements and organizations eschewing violence as unrealistic . . . theorists of world order have noted the common inability of both capitalist and communist thought to contemplate serious alternatives to the present creaky system of nation-states" (Scott 1983, 355). Marxism in theory transcends the nation-state model, but it has yet to prove itself in practice.

Although inability to move beyond the nation-state model is limiting, we cannot subsequently assume that global institutions and planning will answer all of societies' ills. However, "contemporary small-scale societies have reminded us that it is simply not the case that the large-scale bureaucratic state is the only viable form of social organization" (Scott 1983, 357). Scott believes that "the issues of peace and of significant social change . . . are in the long run inseparable from the discipline of a nonviolent practice in social change" (1983, 364). Nonviolence as a serious strategy and method of action is not on the agenda of liberals or liberationists.

Transformationism, somewhat new and untested, is based in the philosophy of the new paradigm. It focuses on imaging a new future, defining world problems as human caused, and the increasing delegitimization of war. The strategies and actions of nonviolence, both at the individual and group level, are considered paramount. Methods of direct nonviolent action drawn from Gandhi and other actors of nonviolence are studied and lived. Transformationism attempts to move beyond the nation-state model to test new forms of small community government.

Transformationists' strengths lie in broadening the methodology for change to include nonviolence and realizing that to change society, individuals must change. Their theories are more encompassing of what it means to be human; they include mysticism, spirituality, and aesthetics in the discussion. However, they must resist the temptation to move solely into the realm of analysis of the individual. The liberationist critique of societal institutions is extremely powerful; transformationists must acknowledge and include these analyses in their arguments to balance what is sometimes an overemphasis on the role of the individual in bringing about peace.

The next chapter focuses on the power of the liberationist critique, which exposes the underlying violent structures of society.

3. A Liberationist Critique

If the study of peace is to be meaningful, we must examine the underlying violent structures of our society and the resultant conditions. For this to happen, structured critiques of patriarchy, capitalism, and the consequences of the nation-state system must become central in peace studies. Peace educators must closely examine and come to grips with the premises, definitional modes, and relationships of these violent structures; they must face and address them. The Marxist and feminist liberationist perspectives provide extremely powerful analyses of violent structures and conditions. Students in peace studies must be made aware of and exposed to these radical analyses. Liberationist perspectives cannot be ignored.

Escalations of peacelessness in the world today are myriad, and range from the personal to the global and beyond. It is useful to group them into two main forms of violence: direct and indirect. The discussion of direct violence that follows will deal with war, while the section on structural, or indirect violence, will focus on two main subjects—patriarchy and capitalism.

Though some argue violence may at times be called for in personal self-defense, it is also plausible to argue that nothing can generally be achieved through violence as policy. Although one violent act might temporarily appease a particular circumstance, it breeds further violence and misery in the long term. Violence leads to violence. As Einstein's popular saying declares: "You cannot simultaneously prevent and prepare for war." Or put another way by A. J. Muste, "There is no way to peace, peace is the way." Yet there are those who believe that problems can still be solved through violence. Such attempts have led to the creation of further problems. The superficial appeal of violence is its seeming utility.

The ability or inability to justify war is intimately tied to the perceived relationship between means and ends. To justify war, through whatever context, requires that one separate the means from the ends; only then "can good consequences emerge from evil actions" (Cady 1989, 44). For most pacifists, this separation is not only wholly arbitrary, but dangerous. Means and ends are intimately linked; they are not separate, but different aspects of a particular event (Cady 1989, 44).

Victory as the objective of war is isolated from the means, strategy and tactics leading to mass destruction and violence. "However hard we try to separate means and ends, the results we achieve are extensions of the policies we live; the means we choose reflect the sort of end we seek" (Cady 1989, 48).

We cannot use war to end war, aggression to stop aggression, we cannot kill for peace. We must recognize that lies, violence, rape, murder, and war cannot produce democracy, freedom, and peace. In peace studies, it is of particular importance that the means and ends be congruent. As nonviolent activist David Dellinger said, our methods must be worthy of the ideals we seek to serve (1970, 19). "Every act we perform today must reflect the kind of human relationship we are fighting to establish tomorrow" (Dellinger 1970, 20).

There are many forms of direct violence in the world, the most structured and legitimated of which is war. War, the engagement of state violence, reaches incomprehensible levels of violence and threatens global survival. Its eradication has been the primary concern of peace studies. Though war in the past may have been an effective policy tool, with the technology that we have today, the consequences are becoming ever more uncontrollable and costly. The direct and indirect cost of war is extremely high. "The Presidential Commission on World Hunger estimated that it would cost only $6 billion per year to eradicate malnutrition, an amount equivalent to less than four days' arms expenditure" (Walsh 1984, 15). More than ever, war is a deadly game.

The problem for the proponents of peace studies is to show that abolishing war is a reasonable goal. As Johan Galtung says:

> Abolition of war as an institution is by no means more a priori impossible than the abolition of slavery or the abolition of colonialism. The defenders of all three of these institutions have always invoked the idea that slavery/colonialism/war is intrinsic to "human nature," without ever really contemplating whether the institution is equally intrinsic to the persons bought and sold (slaves), the peoples possessed and sometimes dispossessed (the colonials), or the countless victims of war (1988, 253).

It is the suppression of the reality of victims that supports the belief that war is rational. The pursuance of war must be based on lies. The United States is increasingly gaining a militaristic reputation as a warrior nation. As Barbara Ehrenreich so aptly points out, when the Berlin Wall fell and it seemed we no longer had communism to fight, we heated up the "war" on drugs. What should have been a focus on poverty and shame "became a new occasion for martial rhetoric and muscle flexing" (Ehrenreich 1990, 100). Our society is preoccupied with aggression, bullying, power, and destruction.

Though the outbreak of war and other direct violence presents direct threats to lives, it is the underlying condition that must be addressed—injustice. War is characterized by its limited duration. Direct violence is intentional and goal centered, and therefore is usually quick and obvious. Yet, the distortive main structures of society have characteristics that inherently harm people. Economic injustices, e.g., social practices, may be doing enormous harm at varying levels to all citizens. Barbara Deming once said:

> Bullets and bombs are not the only means by which people are killed. If a society denies to certain of its members food or medical attention, or a political voice, the sense of their own worth, the freedom to exercise their talent—this, too, is waging war of a kind. . . . To confront the truth about the actions we as a nation have taken, abroad and at home, and not simply to think about them but to let ourselves feel what the human cost has been—so that we have to cry out and then have to change—that is our only hope. (Deming 1986)

This is a tall task, but one that all peace studies programs face, and challenge each day, in some way. Structural violence, particularly in the forms of patriarchy and capitalism, has become endemic in modern nation states and shape the categories of reality for most people.

Patriarchy, the social, economic, cultural domination of women by men, is one of the main institutions that sustains and legitimates structural violence today. It has existed throughout time under every form of economic system. Patriarchy seeks to trivialize, domesticate, and silence women's voices and knowledge. Women may easily be the largest oppressed and historically the most exploited group extant. In the same vein, racism is an institution causing vast harm to an enormous number of humans. Unfortunately, millions of people fall under both categories and get a double dose of exploitation and hatred. However, we can argue that patriarchy is the underlying, preexisting base institution of structural violence.

The plight of women in this so-called advanced age reveals the far reaching and deep cutting effects of a patriarchal system of oppression. To help them remain in control, men have created a false dichotomy of attributes. Characteristics naturally common to both sexes have been divided and identified as "male" or "female." Men are strong, aggressive, decisive, powerful, and rational; women are weak, complying, indecisive, meek, and irrational. These false divisions allow patriarchy to survive.

Women all over the world are oppressed and exploited. Many statistics could be given on the abuse of women: a woman is physically abused every 18 seconds by a husband or lover. They earn 60 cents on the dollar compared to men in the same situation. Brock-Utne quotes a United Nations statistic that says "women are doing two-thirds of the work in the world (paid and unpaid), receive ten per cent of the salaries, and own one per cent of the property" (1987, 58). Women are still often treated like slave labor. And in many developing countries, being a woman has little value apart from producing male offspring. Ultrasound clinics abound in countries such as India so that women can abort female fetuses and try again for a boy. In many cases, because women cannot afford an ultrasound, they end up killing the girl babies after they are born—an act that has become culturally and, in most cases, legally accepted. While patriarchy is arguably the oldest form of structural violence, a more modern form that also has a deep-cutting global impact is capitalism.

Under capitalism, patriarchy takes on particular new forms of structural violence. Capitalism as an economic system is characterized by private or corporate ownership of capital goods and production, by investments determined by private decision rather than by state control, and by prices, production, and the distribution of goods that are determined mainly by competition in a so-called "free market." Capitalism is an inherently predatory system, which once had a liberating influence but is fast becoming self-defeating.

On the rise of capitalism, Somerville (1975) explains that early on, capitalism was seen as a liberator from serfdom and paternalism. In its earliest stages, capitalism's competition had socially progressive effects; it broke down the traditional restrictions of feudalism and stimulated individuals to pursue their interests to the extent of their ability and resources. Yet, as the technology of production became more massive and complex, the degree of equality of opportunity to compete decreased in proportion, yet the pressure to compete mounted.

Proponents of capitalism necessarily support the premise that everyone has an equal opportunity to succeed in a free-market economy, assuming they are hard-working and persevere. If one fails, it is because they have less ability and determination. But separating the cultural, sociological, racial, emotional, historical, psychological, and physical factors from the economic simply gives us a distorted picture of reality. Peace educators must challenge this myth of inequality due solely to unequal abilities. As Michael Lewis points out in *The Culture of Inequality,*

> [T]he presumption of equal opportunity leads many people to justify the existence of social and economic inequality by reference to assumed unequal personal endowments of character and competence. —To be poor, to have suffered disadvantage, [is] taken to mean failure to make the most of an abundance of chances; through sloth, venality, or simple ineptitude, one [has] not exerted sufficient productive effort, and having done less than one might, one [has] done ill (1978, 185).

In reality, the vast majority of people enter the work force where they can, instead of where they would, and most have very limited mobility from that point. "Primitive equality was ended by private property, which led to the differential personal ownership of wealth" (Wilber 1983, 265). The increasing affluence of some under this system has caused increasing scarcity for others. Norman Thomas expresses this point concisely: "The involuntary poverty of [humankind] in the face of its collective power to acquire abundance is a disgrace to society and a deep injury to [humankind]" (Cohen 1972, 515).

Since capitalism relies on exploited labor, it naturally sets up a conflict of interest between those who have and those who do not. Originally, Marx and Engels depicted this class conflict by describing the true relations between the owners of the means of production and the proletariat. Though capitalism has changed in ways unforeseen since Marx and Engels, the dichotomy between oppressors and oppressed still exists, but in new forms. "Henry C. Wallich, the conservative Yale economist, is worried about what would happen if the G.N.P. stopped growing: 'Growth is a substitute for equality of income. So long as there is growth there is hope, and that makes large income differential tolerable'" (Lakey 1987, 70).

While those who "have" may think themselves happy, their oppression harms not only the oppressed, but also themselves. Paulo Freire, in his historical work, *Pedagogy of the Oppressed* speaks to this issue:

> The oppressors do not perceive their monopoly on having more as a privilege that dehumanizes others and themselves. They cannot see that, in the egoistic pursuit of having as a possessing class, they suffocate in their possessions and no longer are; they merely have. For them, having more is an inalienable right, a right they acquired through their own "effort," with their "courage to take risks." If others do not have more, it is because they are incompetent and lazy, and worst of all is their unjustifiable ingratitude towards the "generous gestures" of the dominant class. Precisely because they are "ungrateful" and "envious," the oppressed are regarded as potential enemies who must be watched. (1970, 45)

This being/having dichotomy is discussed at length in Erich Fromm's *To Have or To Be?* Fromm argues that attaining material wealth and comfort promised to bring unrestricted happiness, but didn't deliver. Though we are a nation of radical hedonists, we are notoriously unhappy. The reason? "Greed and peace preclude each other" (Fromm 1976, xxviii). We are too busy "having" to give attention to our "being." In fact, we are often defined and define ourselves by what we have. This emphasis has created a pattern of over-consumption and consequent waste unparalleled in history.

Few people in the United States realize what a rich country we are, and how radically different our lifestyle is from the majority of the world's population. It is worth taking a look at what we would have to do to our lives to make them comparable to the typical person's life in the Third World:

(1) Take the furniture out of your home. Leave a few old blankets, a kitchen table, maybe a wooden chair. You've never had a bed, remember? (2) Throw out your clothes. Each person in the family may keep the oldest suit or dress, a shirt or blouse. The head of the family has the only pair of shoes. (3) All kitchen appliances have vanished. Keep a box of matches, a small bag of flour, some sugar and salt, a handful of onions, a dish of dried beans. Rescue those moldy potatoes from the garbage can: That is tonight's meal. (4) Dismantle the bathroom, shut off the running water, take out the wiring and the lights and everything that runs by electricity. (5) Take away the house and move the family into the toolshed. (6) By now, all the other houses in the neighborhood have disappeared; instead there are shanties—for the fortunate ones. (7) Cancel all magazines. Throw out the books. You won't miss them—you are now illiterate. One radio is now left for the whole shantytown. (8) No more mail carrier, firefighter, government services. The two-classroom school is three miles away, but only two of your seven children attend anyway, and they walk. (9) No hospital, no doctor. The nearest clinic is now 10 miles away with a midwife in charge. You get there by bus or by bicycle, if you're lucky enough to have one. (10) Throw out your bankbooks, stock certificates, pension plans, insurance policies. You now have a net worth of $5. (11) Get out and start cultivating your three acres. Try hard to raise $300 in cash crops because your landlord wants one-third and your moneylender 10 percent. (12) Find some way for your children to bring in a little extra money so you have something to eat most days. But it won't be enough to keep bodies healthy—so lop off 25 to 30 years of your life (Utne Reader Jan./Feb. 1991, 120-21).

This guided visualization starkly uncovers the incredible differences in lifestyle that go unnoticed by so many of us (myself included) most of the time.

Political philosopher Alfredo Rocco asked the question in 1925, and we must ask it again today: "If the state is created for the welfare of its citizens, how can it tolerate an economic system which divides the population into a small minority of exploiters, the capitalists, on the one side, and an immense multitude of exploited, the working people, on the other" (Cohen 1972, 320)? When capitalism became imperialistic, the entire world became its arena for exploitation. This development, as Somerville points out, is the most dangerous consequence of the private profit motive.

> Here, the most precious natural resources to be found in one country can become owned or economically controlled by a small group of people in another country. As legal slavery made individual human beings into objects of sale in the market place, legal capitalism made the natural resources of whole countries objects of sale in the investment market (Somerville 1975, 69-70).

Third World countries, in need of any kind of economic assistance, sell their precious resources, their land, and agree to take our garbage and toxic waste out of desperation. Their people work in our plants for pittance, and we pat ourselves on the back for helping the disadvantaged while we raze their rainforests and sell them chemicals too hazardous to pass for use in the U.S. If it were not for our greed, extreme over-consumption of the *world's* resources—if we actually shared what we have (including knowledge) and stopped taking what everybody else has—the rest of the world might be miraculously transformed.

When we look at capitalism closely, we uncover the fact that it is a form of war. Its competitive nature sets up a concealed dichotomy of us against them, the winners and the losers. Many people don't understand or don't care to admit that in capitalism, there *must be losers*. It is that simple. Capitalism is economic warfare. We harbor resources, scope out the enemy, plan coups and hostile takeovers. The fall out of this war is that we allow people to die of hunger in the streets while others, maybe two blocks away, drive a $500,000 car. The essentially warlike attitude of capitalism is exemplified in the words of Donald Trump: "My style of deal-making is quite simple and straightforward. I aim very high, and then I just keep pushing and pushing and pushing to get what I'm after" (1987, 45). "I don't do it for the money. I've got enough, much more than I'll ever need. I do it to do it.... I like making deals, preferably big deals. That's how I get my kicks" (Trump 1987, 1). "I enjoy combat. I enjoy fighting my enemies. I like beating people and winning" (Plasken 1989, 10). One can see the essentially competitive, violent, exploitative, and warlike nature of capitalism in his words.

The main problem with capitalism is that it is driven by profit, greed, and domination instead of human need. "As you read this, forty children per minute will die from starvation while $15 million per minute is spent on weapons" (Goldstein and Kornfield 1987, 163). Shocking, but not surprising. The decisions which create such mad situations are based on a political and economic mentality of domination. In the words of Bowles and Gintis,

> Modern capitalism is characterized by a set of highly advanced technological possibilities played out in the confines of a backward and retarding set of social relationships. . . . Inflation, commodity shortages, unemployed workers, and unmet social needs all attest to the growing inability of capitalism to meet people's needs

for material comfort, economic security, and social amenity. . . . Capitalism is an irrational system, standing in the way of further social progress. It must be replaced (1983, 388, 392).

Capitalism, one of the most powerful and brutal forms of structural violence, is an inherently unjust system.

A balancing approach to the extremes of patriarchy and capitalism may be found in socialist-feminism. This perspective preserves the basic rights of all human beings regardless of sex, race, or desire to compete. Though there are disagreements in the field of socialist-feminism, as with any field, we can find general things on which most socialist-feminists agree. Two main premises are that: "1. Sexism has a life of its own. It has existed throughout human history, under every economic system. 2. Capitalism determines the particular forms of sexism in a capitalist society. The subjugation of women contributes to capitalists' domination of society" (Jagger and Rothenberg 1984, 152). The oppression of women by men is paralleled by the oppression of the worker by the capitalist. The lack of women's control over their bodies is paralleled by their lack of control over the means of production. Men must dominate women because women have the immense power of reproduction. In the end, what is needed is *democratic* socialism, not the totalitarian socialist governments we have seen to date.

In the forefront of socialist-feminism is the work of Barbara Ehrenreich, who finds the capitalist/patriarchy paradigm already obsolete. She believes that individual companies and industries no longer care about reproducing the labor force (one of the main arguments of patriarchal-capitalism). What they are concerned with is consumers, and reproducing a growing market of consumers. Whereas previously, the patriarchal-capitalist system may have busied itself with keeping housewives reproducing the labor force and producing unpaid labor at home, what is now of concern is that a society of singles has potentially greater buying power than a husband-wife one income family.

For Ehrenreich, the climate of capitalism is growing and changing so rapidly that the old paradigm of patriarchal-capitalism no longer holds great power. The basic concepts of their theory—the state, the economy, the family—are all changing so rapidly that a new paradigm is called for (Ehrenreich 1989, 345). So where do socialist-feminists go from here if their old paradigm no longer holds water? Ehrenreich says that the most meaningful and powerful vantage points are still feminist and socialist (or, rather, Marxist) and, therefore, they should not be abandoned. However, socialist-feminists should be hesitant about buying into a new, similarly "scientific" paradigm in such a rapidly changing climate. In all, the theories of socialist-feminism provide a guiding light as to why and how our systems need to be reformed.

The liberalism of peace studies, because it seeks gradual reform within the system, is not having that great of an impact in bringing about peace. It does not seek to uproot the underlying institutions causing tremendous structural violence in our society. We need a more powerful critique, such as those provided by feminist and Marxist analyses of patriarchy and capitalism. Although these critiques are valid and insightful, they too often rely on the reductionism or downward causation based in the materialistic critique of the Newtonian-Cartesian paradigm. The problem is that we are not solely causally determined by the oppressive institutions of our culture. Though we are shaped to a degree by social structures, we ourselves have psychological inadequacies and disturbances that in turn affect society.

The transformationist perspective argues that to bring about peace, one must transform oneself as one works to transform society. In so doing, the transformationist critique adds to the liberationist critique emergent properties, thus filling out the analysis and creating a more holistic perspective. (The liberationist perspective that comes closest to and at times, overlaps, transformationism is Critical Theory, discussed in Chapter 2). Individual transformation cannot wait for the transformation of socio-economic institutions or solidification of a more humane culture. The crises we face today, though themselves complex and exacerbated by political, social, and economic factors, stem fundamentally from our own psyches. Because the state of the world reflects the state of our minds, the causes of our current dilemmas must be sought within us (Walsh 1984, 42).

4. Toward A Transformationist Approach

The literature review revealed that the peace studies discussion lies on the liberal end of the spectrum, and, as we will see in the next chapter, the program review reflects this. Though some researchers and educators are beginning to step into the liberationist (focusing on structural violence and reconstruction of the state through more humane institutions) and transformationist (focusing on personal nonviolence and spirituality and moving beyond the nation-state model) realms, the vast majority of debate, development, and educating in peace studies falls within the liberal tradition.

For the last 200 years, we have identified positions on the appropriate role of the state as left-middle-right or liberal-moderate-conservative positions. This patterning has spilled over to influence our social, economic, and cultural lives; it permeates the policy debates of our educational system. Our thought has become fixated on this dualistic model. Though peace studies programs and research in the liberal tradition present positive efforts to work for peace, the liberalism of peace studies is, frankly, not having that much of an impact in political arenas. Liberalism seeks gradual reform within the existing institutions and framework of society. Liberal peace education does not cut deeply enough as a critique of the core institutions and practices breeding violence in our society. Until this happens, the possibility for positive peace remains dubious.

Furthermore, Americans seem to have lost confidence in the liberal model of education and are increasingly turning to a conservative, and at times, reactionary, model. If liberalism is losing ground as a critical tradition that can justify the quest toward world peace, what can we turn to? The problem is this: If we begin our analysis from the assumption of the nation state as primary actor, and our discourse stays within the liberal to conservative debate, we will continue to end up in the conundrums of these positions. Looking at the world through this template is stifling. We need to step beyond the boundaries of the liberal to conservative model, to free ourselves from that limited picture. We are living in unprecedented times. What we need is an unprecedented model.

The transformationist perspective provides a new way of thinking, of looking at the world. Transformationism is capable of addressing the difficulties and problems found in the approaches of liberalism and liberationism. It presents needed new analyses, capable of grasping new realities which liberalism and liberationism fail to do. This process has the capacity to keep our commitments to rational, scientific thought, open communication, and focus on problems and individuals, while simultaneously opening up creative new possibilities. It is fruitful in that it can change the discussion entirely, opening up new perspectives and solutions. This new perspective is a systematic and disciplined critique. It is not anti-intellectual; it is, as we will discover, anti-separatist.

A discussion of epistemological issues follows, with an exploration of our conceptions of knowledge and science and our intellectual assumptions. Rather than focusing on conditions, as the liberationist critique has, this argument investigates the way we look at the world—our assumptions, knowledge, and beliefs. It is, in effect, a critical epistemology of a new sort. To unlock the foundational premises that (unintentionally) provided the building blocks for development of the extensive structural violence previously described, we must turn to an analysis of the traditional modes of thinking, represented in liberalism and liberationism, and founded in the thought of Descartes and Newton, among others. This analysis will be followed by a proposal of transformationist alternatives.

Evolving Beyond the Old Paradigm

The definitional premises on which much of our institutionalized structural violence was built can be found in the ideas and guidelines set forth by the current, or as it is sometimes called, the old, paradigm. Though the old paradigm is not the entire basis of our problems, it did prepare us to justify our actions. Founded in the thought of Descartes, Newton, and Bacon, the traditional paradigm is linear, deterministic, and reductionistic. Basically a materialist philosophy, this view puts forth that things can be explained according to their smallest components. Its model is mechanistic, and it tends to compartmentalize, fragment, and isolate things in order to study them. Prediction is a main concern of this paradigm. Based on Descartes' cogito, it separates mind and body. Rationality and intellect are held as superior.

Though the old paradigm seems to have carried its own seeds of destruction, it does leave us with some valid methods and ideas. Micro-determinism is a useful tool, and empirical observation and the inductive and deductive methods have brought us to the advanced level of technology and science that we enjoy today. Also careful analysis, advanced reasoning skills, and critical, skeptical thinking are positive contributions of the old paradigm. However, against Descartes' intentions, these have been put into the science of the capitalist structures. In fact, one of the main reasons we face the vast number of problems we do today is belief, indeed, complete faith in the Newtonian-Cartesian paradigm and consequent over-emphasis on reductionist thought.

With its focus on linearity, determinism, and mechanistics, this paradigm has laid the foundation for a set of beliefs and values that are warped. Capitalism, born and nurtured under this paradigm, values aggression, expansion, profit, exploitation, competition, and power, and devalues cooperation, voluntary simplicity, conservation, synergy, intuition, and loving-kindness. The Cartesian paradigm encourages an essentially exploitative relationship with the earth and with other living creatures. Focus on analytic rationality and "yang values" has helped to bring us to the crisis we now face.

> This emphasis, supported by the patriarchal system and further encouraged by the dominance of the sensate culture during the past three centuries, has led to a pro-

found cultural imbalance which lies at the very root of our current crisis—an imbalance in our thoughts and feelings, our values and attitudes, and our social and political structures . . . the strikingly consistent preference for yang values, attitudes, and behavior patterns has resulted in a system of academic, political, and economic institutions that are mutually supportive and have become all but blind to the dangerous imbalance of the value system that motivates their activities (Capra 1982, 39).

Our evolution, which has been largely one of intellect and reason, seems on a collision course with itself. We have neglected the development of intuitive and cooperative abilities, as well as the legitimation of subjectivity. As Willis Harman points out, "the Western neglect of the realm of subjective experience has had serious consequences in our confusion about values. For it is ultimately in this realm of the subjective, the transcendent, and the spiritual that all societies have found the basis for their deepest value commitments and sense of meaning" (1988, 29).

Harman argues that our culture centers on economic decisions, and a person's worth is judged according to his/her economic value. Our most sacred beliefs and values hinge on economic/financial matters. This bizarre emphasis has created a society that is verging on the insane. While we cannot afford to feed, clothe, or shelter our own people, we can spend billions on nuclear arsenals, advertising, and recreation. If the old paradigm fostered capitalist practices, what is its relation to communism?

If capitalism causes so many problems, what do we turn to? The reader might at this point be wondering, communism? There has yet to be a single truly communist government. Bishop Dom Helder Camara once said "I brought food to the hungry, and people called me a saint; I asked why the people were hungry, and people called me a communist." Just as communism has done to capitalism, capitalism has "demonized" the enemy. This separation is false from both sides of the spectrum. We must look at others and ourselves in a more integrated, realistic perspective. To the question of what is next after capitalism, there is no easy answer. Capitalism, the cause of oppression, fragmentation, and dehumanization, fosters the natural human desire of greed. Communism and socialism frustrate greed and ideally provide basic human services for all, but also may lead to oppression, fragmentation, and alienation.

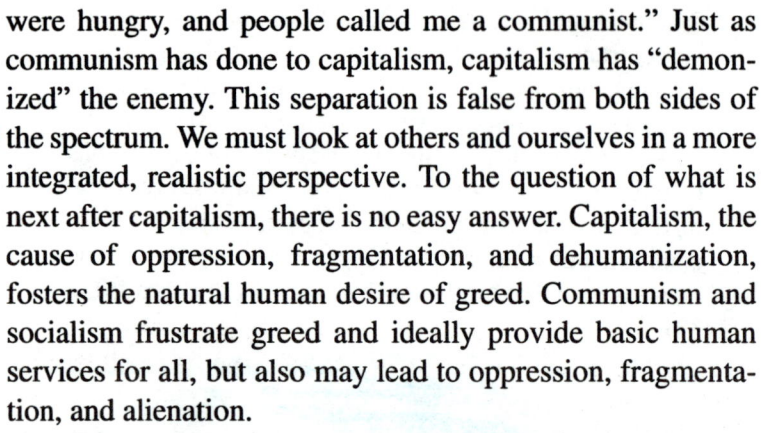

Like capitalism, the forms of communism that exist today are not pure. There has yet to be a strictly Marxist society as Marx envisioned it. The communism of the former Soviet Union is state capitalism, and therefore has some of the same problems as our capitalistic society. There is an elite class with special privileges and access; and a consequent division of classes resulting in some degree of alienation, oppression, and fragmentation. There are also many problems with meeting the basic needs of many of its people. Even in countries that boast equity and freedom for their people, we find inequality and enslavement. In reality, Marxist theory, based on dialectical materialism, is closely tied to the Newtonian-Cartesian paradigm. In fact, one scholar even refers to the old paradigm as the Cartesian-Newtonian-Marxist paradigm, and argues that all materialistic philosophies (including capitalism and Marxism) have or will collapse (Singh 1988, 144). Therefore, the answer to many of these injustices may not be capitalist, Marxist or otherwise. "The ultimate solution to unfreedom, then, is neither Humanistic-Marxist nor Freudian-Conservative, but Buddhistic: satori, moksha, wu, release, awakening, metanoia" (Wilber 1983, 334).

Though the solution to our problems may not be Buddhistic per se, it definitely lies in the realm of the transpersonal. As Richard Quinney points out, "Oppression in this world is caused by selves that are not spiritually aware, by those who live by greed, fear, egoism, and the craving for power over others" (1988, 71). Only when we are able to get beyond the small self and its ego will there be an equitable distribution of power. The main problem in our political/economic systems, then, is not the amount of freedom, oppression, or exploitation, but that we are ruled by our egos. As long as we are being driven by the desires of the ego, we will never create a society in which equity and equality prevail.

> Economic equality is "beyond the endurance of the democratic type" of person. And, I would add, the socialist type as well. The democratic and the socialist ego are still egos, and egos by structure house the *tendency* and the *power* for exploitation, repression, and oppression. As a frightening Czechoslovakian saying has it, "In democracy, man exploits man [sic]; in communism, it's the other way around" (Wilber 1983, 285).

The important point is this: "It is impossible to create a well-working society on a knowledge base which is fundamentally inadequate, seriously incomplete, and mistaken in basic assumptions" (Harman 1988, 101).

We cannot use old ways of thinking to solve problems that have been created because of the old ways of thinking (Zimmerman 1988, 199). To secure peace, it is not enough to overthrow the main institutions causing structural violence. The revolution must come at an individual level. In fact, how could the institutions crumble without major changes in individuals? And even if they did fall, the institutions replacing them would be inadequate if they did not reflect truly profound change. We find that there is something deeper than structural violence at work. There is personal violence, and suffering.

According to Buddhism, suffering is an inherent part of life. Even if there were no human beings, suffering would still exist due to natural disasters and the hierarchies and violence found in nature. I have discussed many problems—the direct violence of war, the structural violence of patriarchy and capitalism, and the system of thought represented by the old paradigm. What do all of these problems have in common? They all boil down to vast suffering, not only of people, but of animals, plants, trees—the earth herself. We have seen that there are systems of oppression that cause many problems, but do all the problems we have examined have a common cause? A single basis? Is all of the suffering caused by these problems discussed coming from one place? Yes. These problems are all human caused. Focusing specifically on suffering may surprise some people and be perceived as over-emphasizing the negative. However, as Buddhist-feminist Charlene Spretnak once said, "When there is a heavy layer of denial, simply telling the truth seems shocking." And the truth is that human beings cause vast suffering. Herein is where transformationism breaks away from liberationism.

While liberationism argues that the root causes of suffering lie in oppressive social and economic institutions with their distortive human relationships and accompanying forms of false consciousness, transformationism argues that even while we are shaped by social conditions, our individual psychological disturbances also lie at the root of our global problems. Though institutions cause suffering, individuals within institutions also cause suffering. This causality is not one-way, but two-way; it is reciprocal and self-perpetuating. Our "global problems reflect our collective psychological disturbances" (Walsh 1984, xvii). Transformationists argue that our crises, though "complex and exacerbated by political, social and economic factors, stem fundamentally from our own psyches" (Walsh 1984, 42). To the extent that our current crises are human caused, we need to search out these causes in human behavior and psychological forces. We cannot only look to transform our social structures; we must also, and more elementally, look to transform ourselves.

Each of the major (and minor) problems that exist today are a manifestation of the psychological problems rooted not only in irrational and contradictory social conditions, but in our psyches. If the cause of these problems lies not only in institutions, but ultimately in each individual, then the solution is apparent. Though oppressive institutions must be transformed, so must we transform ourselves if we are to eradicate these problems. If we want peace in the world, we must first have peace within ourselves. "We are aggressive, brutal, competitive, and we build a society which is equally competitive, brutal, and violent" (Krishnamurti 1972, 31). Ideally, if we were inwardly loving, considerate, and caring, there would be no wars. This may seem a simple conclusion, but let us stay with it. We have discussed the oppressive institutions of patriarchy and capitalism. Do the aggressive and brutal nature of these systems not reflect our individual psyches? Are they not a creation of our collective psychological (and emotional, intellectual, and social) disturbances? If somehow we were each noncompetitive, egalitarian, loving, generous, and so on, could there be such things as capitalism and patriarchy?

Nagler explains that there is a reason all of the previous attempts to find a stable concept of peace have failed, why there has been no lasting, or strong peace concept paradigm:

> These conceptual failures are inevitable as long as it is not recognized that the sources of war and, consequently,

peace are within the human individual. Individuals can overcome the ultimate cause of war within themselves and convert it to an equally titanic force—how else explain a phenomenon like Gandhi. Marianne Moore's "In Distrust of Merits" encapsulates this insight perfectly: "There never was a war that was not inward; I must fight till I have conquered in myself what causes war" (Goebel and Nelson 1988, 133).

"The threats to our survival can be traced to psychological and social immaturities, inauthenticities, and pathologies . . . faulty beliefs, fear, defensiveness, and so on . . ." (Walsh 1984, 43). Much of what we do as individuals is directly or indirectly violent—speech, gestures, actions, innuendos; however, the greatest violence may result from our inaction. "The outer world reflects our inner wars, paralyses, and guilt. Mostly we have sinned by omission—not so much by cheating or unkindnesses, but by failing to act, by tolerating wrongs" (Ferguson 1980, 424).

Though humans have caused the major problems of structural violence we now face, we need not condemn ourselves as hopeless as a species. We each hold within us incredible powers of transformation and change. People become sober, stop smoking, they fast—the mind is an extremely powerful tool. There should be no reason individuals cannot bring about peace collectively. Individual peace is a pathway to world peace. After all, angry, violent people fighting each other will never bring about world peace. The crises that fill the world today can be viewed as symptoms—global symptoms—of our collective psychological disturbances. As Roger Walsh says, "The task facing us is two-fold. One is to work to relieve the suffering in the world. The other is to work to relieve the psychological causes, starting first within ourselves, that contribute to this suffering. The challenge then, is not only to contribute but also to learn and mature in the process" (Walsh 1985, xviii). This is part of the work of peace studies programs.

Being Peace

If peace studies programs are to embrace the study and search for peace in its wholeness, individuals must be willing to work at actually being, becoming peace themselves. Though there are many other necessary aspects to studying and bringing about peace, we cannot hope for or envision peace if we are not willing to try to bring peace to our own lives. "Peace education rests on the assumption that the way to change social systems riddled by violence and committed to war is to change oneself. Until people change one by one they are not going to change by the thousands. . . . Peace educators can best become change agents by paying attention to the changes they themselves go through as they address the issues of war and peace and listening carefully to the concerns of others" (Harris 1988, 158). Or, as Gandhi tells us "If one does not practice non-violence in one's personal relations with others and hopes to use it in bigger affairs, one is vastly mistaken . . ." (Merton 1965, 26). We have to start working for peace in our own minds, by creating it in our own lives. We cannot teach peace or be "peace activists" if we are not each working to be peace.

If part of the answer is to be found in trying to bring about inner, individual peace, then it makes sense to ask how this relates to peace studies programs. After all, peace is not passive. How can a way of life, a tone of living, be transmitted? How does one understand what peace is at a deep, fundamental level? By being it, through living it. What we need to help students examine is not only the conditions of suffering, but living peace, being peace. We need to ask students, "How can we be peace?" What is the essence of being peace? Since the phenomenological process is very effective in uncovering the essence of a thing, I will follow its guidelines for inquiry. This phenomenological process involves trying to analyze the experience of peace and find examples of being peace.

Peace manifests itself in various, subtle ways. It does not come quickly, but emerges gently and slowly. Peace often is a precarious experience. It is similar to a bird lighting on your outstretched hand. It does not come because of your striving, diligence, or passion. Rather, it is a gift. When it comes, if you try to control it, change its course, or manipulate it in any way, it flies away. If you get too excited, too passionate, it flies away. Peace comes to you, and leaves, effortlessly, gracefully. Experiencing peace is accomplished best through *wu wei*, active nonaction. In doing nothing, everything gets done. By not actively seeking out experiences, everything is experienced.

Often, peace comes to you when the senses are appeased. In other words, it begins physically. If you are hungry, thirsty, or in pain, you are less likely to be visited by peace. (However, maybe for someone who has practiced meditation extensively or has a natural mind/body control, any mind/body state is one in which peace may be present.) But for most "ordinary" people, peace is more likely to be experienced when the senses are nourished. Part of this physical condition is the activity of the brain.

When the mind (the emergent aspect of the brain) is clear, relaxed, and unworried, one is most ready to experience peace. If your mind is in the present, focusing on the moment, you are most likely to experience authentic peace. I say authentic peace because if one's mind wanders in daydreaming, or dwells on some fond memory of the past, or plans some pleasant future event, there may be a type of peace experienced. But that peace is a dreamy, altered state that is similar to a drug. It is pleasant for a period of time, but when you return to the present, nothing has changed or been transformed. It was a pleasant trip, but now you are back in reality. Authentic experiences of peace are transformative, even if only in some small way. How is one transformed by an authentic peace experience? Does experiencing peace make one more likely to experience it again?

Experiences of peace, being, *living* peace, bring about a calm in most situations. At times, being peace means fighting for a belief or cause, but most experiences of peace are ones of calm contemplation, or quiet joy. Being peace is living in a state of equilibrium. It is leading a balanced life in every way, including correct consumption, livelihood, and speech. It means finding a balance between time reserved for yourself, and donating time to help others. If we contemplate people, groups, and movements working at "being peace," what commonalities will we discover?

Gandhi, Mother Theresa, Martin Luther King, Jr., the spiritual leaders over time—Jesus, Buddha, the Gnostics—nonviolent peace activists such as David Dellinger, Barbara Deming, and A.J. Muste, the women at Greenham Common, peace corps volunteers, organizations such as the Buddhist Peace Fellowship, Amnesty International, Greenpeace, the Women's International League for Peace and Freedom, and the United Nations—what do these people, groups, and movements have in common? What do they want? Obviously what they want is peace and justice. What they have in common is that they care. They share a deep concern for human life and the quality of human life. Also, they are all courageous. They face a tremendous up-hill battle, yet they forge on just the same. It is also fair to say that they all work for nonviolence, an eradication of violence, an end to fighting.

What *meaning* is there to being peace? Why do all of these people work toward this goal? The most obvious answer is to improve the quality of one's own life. Being peace makes you happy, allows you to experience joy. However, all life is interconnected. Being peace affects not only you, but all those around you—all of society. There are obvious meanings to being peace: preventing and eradicating war, helping others, sharing your talents and wealth, creating a better, healthier environment, working for justice—the list is long. Yet, all of these meanings seem to be the same. The purpose of being peace, its meaning, is to make the world a better place. It is just that simple. What is the meaning of being peace? To make the world a better place.

We have seen that those most successful at being peace and bringing about peace are nonviolent, courageous, and care deeply about others. A common thread is that many of these people mentioned seem selfless. They seemed to have conquered, or come to terms with, suffering in themselves, allowing them to help to alleviate suffering in other people. What is the basis of suffering? How have some of these people gone beyond it? There must be a connection between suffering and the self.

It is apparent that many of these people of peace are not controlled by their egos. Why does the ego cause suffering? The craving desire of the ego can never be satisfied, it is completely insatiable. Although one particular desire might be temporarily quenched, another will well up in its place, and another, and another. . . . All the ego can do for us is lead us on a continuous path of pain, suffering, and dissatisfaction. As Epictetus said, "We are not troubled by things, but by the opinions which we have of things" (Fields et al. 1984, 182).

We tend to become fixated on a dualistic way of thinking and seeing; we dichotomize into good and bad and break things up into opposites. In so doing, we lose sight of the wholeness or commonality underlying these apparent polarities (Walsh 1984, 34-35). Our egos spend vast amounts of time judging and craving.

The desire displayed by our examples of peace people is not for themselves, but for others. It is a desire born out of love. It is not the selfish craving desire born out of ego. What is desire? Have we ever stopped to examine it, to really feel it?

> The wanting mind is itself painful. It's a self-perpetuating habit that does not allow us to be where we are because we are grasping for something somewhere else.... So the force of desire can cloud our minds, bringing distortions and delusion in its wake. As it says in the *Tao Te Ching*, "The secret waits for eyes unclouded by longing" ... When we look, we see that it creates tension, that it is actually painful. We can see how it arises out of our sense of longing and incompleteness, the feeling that we are separate and not whole (Goldstein and Kornfield 1987, 33-37).

What then are we to do about our selfish, craving selves? We can't very well just toss our egos out the window—they have been conditioned and nurtured since birth. According to Wilber, humankind is at the most distressful period of all in the evolution of consciousness, because "the ego is perched midway between total slumber in the subconscious and total enlightenment in the superconscious" (1983, 111). If we are halfway between "plankton and 'God,'" and are periodically pulled in both directions, what are we to do? The answer must come in awareness and understanding.

How did some of these peace people come to conquer their egos and desire? Many of them have strong spiritual backgrounds, and lead spiritual lives. They must have come to some understanding, some realization. To get to that realization, they must have been supremely aware, of themselves, others, and the world. "Our minds are like a balance scale, and as long as we're identified with these judgments and preferences, likes and dislikes, wants and aversions, our minds are continually thrown out of balance, caught in a tiring whirlwind of reactivity" (Goldstein and Kornfield 1987, 18). Peace work, being peace, cannot take place in that "tiring whirlwind of reactivity." An important aspect of being peace must be mindfulness.

In trying to be peace, being aware—mindful—is extremely helpful. If one focuses on the moment, one "operates" from a more stable center, and is less likely to be swayed by problems that arise. In order to understand, "you have to be one with what you want to understand" (Hanh 1987, 37). In other words, being peace requires non-duality; to fully understand something, we must take it up and be one with it (Hanh 1987, 38). Hanh argues that when we become irritated or angry is when we most need to be aware. It is only through awareness that we can truly understand and love. In-the-moment awareness is the method which allows us to have sovereignty over ourselves, to return to our true selves (Hanh 1987, 7). Non-duality dictates that when we are angry, we are anger; the anger and I are one. Because we are anger—we are in it, we are it—we must treat it with care, tenderness, love, and nonviolence. After all, if we cannot be compassionate with ourselves, how can we be compassionate with others (Hanh 1987, 40)? Awareness creates the possibility to look deeply into the nature of our anger, to perceive its roots without the hindrances of emotions, ignorance, or illusion (Hanh 1987, 42). It allows us to recognize ourselves in those with whom we are angry; in so doing, we can understand the suffering of others. Living life in the moment really does have a transformative effect. Only in the moment, in mindfulness, can one transcend the ego and return to the larger Self. In fact, being aware, being present in the moment, is the greatest impetus for self-transcendence.

"In you . . . at this moment is all time and all space. In other words, this moment is all" (Ross 1981, 57). If this is so, it seems that all we really have to do to go beyond our egos is to be in the moment, see things clearly as they are, not through the eyes of our ego, but with pure attentiveness. "Experiences come and go. If we identify with them, claim them as 'me' or 'mine' by judging or clinging, if we stick to any part of the ongoing flow, we don't see that what we call 'me' is constantly being born and dying, is a process of awareness and object coming into being and passing away hundreds of times each minute" (Levine 1979, 5-6). One only need think about this proposition to find that it is true. Our egos keep our minds constantly chattering in the past or the future: "That movie was really bad." "I have to do laundry when I get home." Very rarely do we actually live in the moment. "In Buddhism, the most important precept of all is to live in awareness, to know what is going on" (Hanh 1987, 65). As Ferguson says, "The beginning of personal transformation is absurdly easy. *We only have to pay attention to the flow of attention itself*" (1980, 68). What can help us to reach that state in which we can live in the moment, baring attention to what is happening now? Any of the psycho-technologies (biofeedback, yoga, chanting, and so on) probably would help; but certainly, this is the main purpose of meditation.

"Meditation is to be aware, and to try to help" (Hanh 1987, 11). In practicing meditation, one learns, by whichever method, to bring one's mind back to the moment gently, over and over again, until it stays naturally. When one's mind is in the moment, not clinging or judging, then one is free simply to be. "Only that bare attention, that non-wantingness that can just be in the moment, has the power to decondition our compulsive reaction to wanting" (Levine 1979, 15-16). The call for mindfulness and meditation is not exclusive to Buddhism or Eastern thought, but can be found in Christianity as well. "What we may need to learn is that merely to look at things as they are, with bare attention, can be a religious act. We are thus enabled to apprehend God's creation as it is, our minds unclouded by egotistical emotions, and so made more aware of God himself [sic]" (Needleman 1980, 109-110). If we do pay attention to the moment, to just being, then what happens to our egos? The realization that people of peace come to may be that ultimately, there is no self. At first, this may sound absurd, but let us explore the issue further. What does it mean to be an individual? Obviously, we are all distinct entities in a physical sense, each having a body. But is there something beyond the physical that we can call "me?" Some would say that the mind or the personality are beyond the physical and therefore, make one an individual beyond the mere physical sense. But do they? More likely, the mind and the personality, which is part of the mind, are simply physical parts of the body that are conditioned.

When one is in the present moment, one notices seeing, hearing, all of the senses, but that is all. There is our body, our environment, our thoughts. Those things are our "self." The ego, the "individual self," is simply a grand illusion that we have created. If we sit quietly and try to describe or define the self, we would find it very difficult. We would naturally point to physical aspects, yet there is something intangible that we would not hesitate to call "me." Alan Watts calls this intangible something "ego," which he says is simply illusion wedded to futility.

The image we have of ourselves, which we create by looking into the mirror, listening to our voices, and to what others have told us we are, is an artificial image, an illusion. We think that we can actually feel our ego, that it is somehow concrete, but that feeling is simply a combination of futile muscular efforts. This false sense of self stems from the combination of this futility and illusion. Watts proposes that what we are is not a group of egos, but that we each are a unified field/organism environment. He believes that we are the whole of our bodies and need the environment to survive; therefore, there should be no separation of self. Things are not only interrelated, but interdependent. A true description of self must include the whole of our bodies, not just our brains; and it also must include the environment in which we find ourselves. We are a unified field, the whole of our bodies, and this unified field is meaningless when taken out of context of its environment. The self is a field within a larger field, meaningless when separated from environment. This definition of self is wholly supported by the latest developments in physics.

This false sense of ego has been carried over the ages because of human's need to feel that they are—that there is a concrete referent that one can point to and call "me." Watts says that this is a dangerous hallucination that gives us a false center of consciousness. It separates us (in here) from them (out there), when, in reality, that separation is completely arbitrary. This creates a combative pattern, i.e. the conquest of nature, conquer space, conquer disease, etc. Gandhi found no-self critical in practicing nonviolence: "If one has pride and egoism, there is no non-violence. Non-violence is impossible without humility" (Merton 1965, 36).

Goldstein and Kornfield clearly explain the no-self concept:

> Our primary delusion, one whose influence pervades all aspects of our lives, is the belief that there is an "I," a self, an ego, that is solid and separate from everything else. But actually this sense of "I" . . . is created entirely by thought and has no substance. . . . But when the mind begins to quiet down, the whole structure begins to slip, and from the ego's point of view that is scary. It's very simple. When thought begins to disappear, who else disappears? We do. Our sense of self is created by our thought process and by the habit of grasping in the mind. If we are not caught up in all our thoughts about our experience, there is simply experience in each moment: just seeing, hearing, smelling, tasting and touching. It is all emptiness, all without self (1987, 145).

The truth of the illusory ego is very threatening. Glimpsing the real Self can be traumatic for the small self or ego. As Harman says, "The ego self is threatened by the existence of the real Self and throws up a variety of smokescreens to block awareness of the true Center. In the end, for integration the ego self must become subservient to the real Self" (1988, 87). Realization that the ego is illusory, non-existent, is a symbolic killing of the ego, which is a form of suicide. Therefore, if "killing the ego," or going beyond it, is necessary for being peace, we can see why we see so little of being peace. It is a very difficult task! Still, in going beyond the ego lies the potential for changing the course of human history.

The idea that the self is an illusion is not in any way restricted to Eastern thought. Einstein explains no-self, and relates it to interconnectedness:

> A human being is part of the whole, called by us the "universe," a part limited in time and space. [One] experiences [oneself], [one's] thoughts and feelings, as something separate from the rest—a kind of optical delusion of [one's] consciousness. This delusion is a kind of prison for us, restricting us to our personal desires and to affec-

tion for a few persons nearest to us. Our task must be to free ourselves from this prison by widening our circle of compassion to embrace all living creatures and the whole of nature (Nagler 1981, 52).

Underneath it all, there is no individuality. Biologically, we are all the same. Spiritually, we are all the same. The biological and spiritual base of all living things is universal. "Going from the ego center to the zero center means seeing things as they are without an artificial separation" (Goldstein and Kornfield 1987, 155). When there is no self, there can be no separation. All is one, or better yet, all is.

The link is this: in going beyond the ego, one finds one's true Self, and in so doing, reunites with all that is. In transcending the self, one is no longer one, but All. In finding one's true Self, one strips away the layers of ego that block the natural flow of peace from within. Being peace emanates naturally from Self, which lies beyond separation and ego. By transcending the small self and returning to Self, one is peace. Therefore, self-transcendence is a crucial part of being peace.

Ultimately, every living thing is related. Life is relationship—with people, things, animals, plants, trees, sky. Without relationship, there is nothing. Everything exists within the framework of relationship. It is what gives us our reality. Krishnamurti explains:

> Relationship is to be; it is existence. You exist because you are related; and it is the lack of understanding of relationship that causes conflict. But relationship is a means to self-discovery. To understand myself, I must understand relationship. Relationship is a mirror in which I can see myself. That mirror can either be distorted, or it can be "as is," reflecting that which is. But most of us see in relationship, in that mirror, things we would rather see; we do not see what is (1954, 120-21).

This reminds us that we must be careful to exercise awareness and mindfulness in our relationships with all things so as not to create stagnant images of things.

Peace studies is concerned ultimately with relationship. Relationships between countries, cultures, societies, individuals, and groups: race/ethnic relations, social class relations, worker/management relations. Peace studies asks, "How can people live and work together?" It seeks to identify the ways in which relationships can become cooperative rather than competitive and exploitative. In realizing that all life is is a series of expanding relationships, we see that nothing is completely isolated. Everything affects everything else; we are in a constant interplay, the flow of life.

Because everything is nothing without relationship, a profound interconnectedness ties all things together. Realizing, experiencing, and understanding this universal connection very deeply is integral to the peace experience. It is not only integral, it is the underlying building block for all actions and intentions of peace. All actions for peace—creating, living, being peace—come out of this universal understanding. It seems that once this oneness is felt, experienced, and conscioused, action for peace necessarily (and naturally) arises. "It's a source of world peace, when we see that we're not separate from the earth but that we all come out of it and are connected with one another. From this sense of connectedness we can commit ourselves to share, to live a life of helpfulness, generosity for the world" (Goldstein and Kornfield 1987, 8).

The realization that "you are the world" is a powerfully transforming phenomenon. Awakening to the fact that nothing exists outside relationship changes the way we look at things. With this understanding, you can look at a piece of paper and see in it the tree, the earth, the cloud, the sun, the rain, the miller, his family, and so on. Once we see that "we are the world," we begin to understand that we can learn of other things through ourselves. As Ross writes from a Buddhist standpoint: "Since All-is-One, knowledge of one's own true nature predicates knowledge of all nature or the universe itself" (1981, 147). Or, as seen in a Christian context, "To know oneself, at the deepest level, is simultaneously to know God" (Pagels 1981, xix).

Again, just as loss of ego is incomprehensible to many people, the idea that we are all interconnected is an unsettling one. People are continually striving to separate themselves from others, to make themselves distinct and unique. Our society would somehow feel we are stifling creativity and keeping people from reaching their potentials if we are taught not to cherish our individuality. This is not so. Imagine the freedom it would create to open yourself up to the realization that you are part of everything, a drop into which the entire ocean of the universe melds? This freedom would allow for maximum innovation and even greater potential. An example of this unleashed creativity can be found in the art of the great Zen masters—their poems, ink drawings, pottery, and so on. Many people argue that God spoke through Mozart and other great composers. Merleau-Ponty writes, "Sometimes one starts to dream about what culture, literary life, and teaching could be if all those who participate, having for once rejected idols, would give themselves up to the happiness of reflecting together" (Green 1973, 289). It is easy to see that opening ourselves up to something beyond our small selves, letting our Selves reflect each other, can bring about miraculous results.

In the end, what is espoused is a spiritual transformation. All major religions hold such seeds of guidance. Each includes as a main concept the idea of going beyond the small self, reuniting with the universe, the One. "When a person re-discovers that [his/her] deepest Nature is one with the All, [s/he] is relieved of the burdens of time, of anxiety, or worry; [s/he] is released from the chains of alienation and separate-self existence" (Wilber 1983, 12). How other than this can we even hope for any sort of peaceful, happy life? Unless we see every living thing as our brothers, sisters, as *ourselves*, we are living in a world of illusion, of separateness, which in the end can only cause more pain, more suffering.

Unity through loss of self then, is what this spiritual process leads to. "True spirituality . . . is an opening, a seeing of the world with a deeper vision that is less self-centered, a vision that sees through dualistic views to the underlying interconnectedness of all life" (Goldstein and Kornfield 1987, 161). If the suffering of life is caused by our craving egos, which are the cause of our separation, then our job is to go beyond our egos and to join again in the ultimate unity with all things. In doing this is our only chance to alleviate suffering. Reaching this state in which we are no longer controlled by our egos, "we remember the bottom line: *We're here to awaken from the illusion of separateness*" (Ram Dass and Gorman 1987, 180). Once the self is seen, felt, heard, touched, realized, as ultimately an illusion, one discovers the beautiful interconnectedness that underlies all life.

Once we realize that life is relationship, a deep care and concern for all life surfaces. We can, in fact, see that a result of this realization of interconnectedness is not only care and concern, but love. A deep, profound, unconditional love of all life. We might look at care and concern as love manifested as responsibility. An important vehicle of being peace is loving-kindness and compassion. What else can shatter the ego so relentlessly and immediately as loving-kindness and compassion for every living thing? And how can one not have compassion and loving-kindness for every living thing once the deep realization of life's interconnectedness occurs?

What is love? Where there is possessiveness and attachment, which breed jealousy, fear, and antagonism, there is no love. This, however, is what many people consider to be love. This sort of 'love' is based on attachment, which is fear of being alone, being empty, and insufficient. As Krishnamurti explains, "Love is passion, which is compassion. Without passion and compassion with its intelligence, one acts in a very limited sense . . . where there is compassion that action is total, complete, irrevocable" (1979, 151-153). When greed and ego drop away, creating space for consideration and understanding, then there is love. Love is necessary to work out our many conflicting problems; for without it, the acquisition of knowledge only increases confusion and leads to further self-destruction (Krishnamurti 1953, 46, 48; also 66). This unconditional love translates into a reverence for all life—an attitude of non-violence, realization of the value and equity of all life, and *metta*, or loving-kindness or compassion. This reverence for all life is readily apparent in the acts of the peace people previously mentioned. "Peace is the practice of love" (Harris 1988, 7). Love may actually have the power of saving the world. As Sri Chin Moi Gosh once said, "When the power of love overcomes the love of power, then there will be true peace."

A natural outcome of this deep love and respect for all life is nonviolence. "Nonviolence is based on the hypothesis that all life is one" (Nagler 1981, 52). If one feels intimately connected to and concerned for all life, one can only be nonviolent. This is a necessary result. One peace researcher found nonviolence to be "the clearest articulation of the deepest values of humanity" (Francis 1990, 12). The paradigm we are currently in rejects such a notion as illegitimate.

Nonviolence and love must reenter science's quest for truth. Peace studies needs "to critique the ethical and logical dimensions of science, to contribute to the rebirth of sciences that pursue truth through love, rather than through the design of weapons of mass destruction . . ." (Crews 1989, 30). The study of the history, assumptions, and theories of nonviolence is crucial in bringing about a new paradigm, and with it, a possibility for peace.

Buddhism has a long history of nonviolence. Galtung notes from his past research that "nomadic societies are by and large less aggressive than industrial societies" and "people in Buddhist societies [are] less aggressive than people in Christian societies" (1985, 155). After all, there has never been a Buddhist war. The Buddhist concept of *ahimsa* encompasses not only personal inner peace, but also a lifestyle of nonviolence. Yet, many people question the efficacy of nonviolence.

We must be careful not to confuse the nonviolence and pacifism of the transformationist approach with passivity. Pacifists are regularly confused with passivists, while the truth is that most pacifists reject passivism (Cady 1989, 12). "Note that compassion and forgiveness do not imply passivity or denial. They do not mean allowing someone to walk all over you or take advantage of you. Nor do they imply a Pollyannaish denial of the existence of destructive motives such as greed and self-aggrandizement. Rather, they represent a denial of the underlying fear and deficiency that power them" (Walsh 1984, 68). In the words of E.F. Schumacher, "It is a grave error to accuse a man who pursues self-knowledge of 'turning his back on society.' The opposite would be more nearly true: that a man who fails to pursue self-knowledge is and remains a danger to society, for he will tend to misunderstand everything that other people say or do, and remain blissfully unaware of the significance of many of the things he does himself" (Walsh 1984, 91). Transformationist peace education calls for increased self-knowledge and psychological growth to be used actively in combatting injustices.

What fears may arise in relation to nonviolence? Doesn't it leave you open, unprotected, vulnerable? Won't people humiliate and abuse you? Gandhi tells us that "The first principle of non-violent action is that of non-cooperation with everything humiliating" (Merton 1965, 29). Through such scholars and activists as Gandhi, Lakey, and Sharp (see Chapter 2), we see that nonviolence is an extremely powerful tool. "We can only speculate about how much more successful nonviolent defense would be were nations to prepare for it with the commitment of resources and energy at levels comparable to current investment in military defense" (Cady 1989, 99). To those who view conquering warism with nonviolence as idealist and naive, we can point to racial integration of public schools, abolition of slavery, and women voting and holding public office as events that also looked exceedingly unlikely not long before they became realities (Cady 1989, 122).

The following quote from Ram Dass and Paul Gorman may be seen as a summary of the relationships discussed in this transformationist philosophy thus far: "Common to all those habits which hinder us is a sense of separateness; we are divided within ourselves and cut off from others. Common to all those moments and action which truly seem to help, however, is the experience of unity; the mind and the heart work in harmony, and barriers between us dissolve" (1987, 223). The transformational process of being peace can be described as follows: We see that life is suffering, much of which is caused by the ego. Through awareness and mindfulness, we discover that the ego is an illusion and there is no "self." This discovery leads us to realize that everything is our relation, and that all life is intimately interconnected. The experience of the ultimate oneness of life produces a profound, unconditional love from which a nonviolent lifestyle of service flows. Such transformation leads to being peace. Being peace means moving beyond separation and working from the unity of life.

The end result of this process of self-realization (or no-self realization) is peace. If each person could go through such a transformation, how could we not have peace? Some Americans may question the need for such a change. They may consider our country, our society, to be at peace already. But how can anyone say that there is peace in the United States (or Sweden, England, and so on) when people die of hunger in our streets? When those very streets are plagued with gunfire? When we abuse our children and wives? We are an advanced nation technologically and in other ways, but we are not a nation at peace. How many of us as individuals could say that our day-to-day lives are filled with loving-kindness and nonviolence? The journey described of inner transformation is not an easy one. It requires faith and courage. However, "people must take risks for peace with the same tenacity and sacrifice that they invest unquestioningly in war and war preparations" (DeBenedetti 1986, 19). Each person is capable of bringing about peace. The choice is up to the individual. "Each person we meet, every situation, every interaction presents us with a choice. We choose whether to set ourselves apart from others or whether to look past the otherness to the self we share; whether to see ourselves as separate and independent from others and the world or affecting and affected by all" (Walsh 1984, 70). Each of us can be and create peace.

This exploration of transformationism completes the examination of the three ideologies of peace studies. I have discussed the theory and value base of liberalism, liberationism, and transformationism, with in-depth analysis of the liberationist critique and the transformationist approach. How do these three ideologies manifest in practice? How do peace studies programs embrace and utilize these ideologies? The next chapter describes and analyzes the various types of peace studies programs in the United States and attempts to answer these, among other, questions.

5. A Review of Peace Studies Programs

A serious discussion of peace studies in the United States today requires not only a grasp of the broad base of literature and ideologies in the field, but also an examination of the nature of the existing programs. I will now present a review of peace studies programs in higher education in the United States, and address: (1) What are the foundational theoretical points of view represented in peace studies programs? (2) What are the prevailing instructional practices? (3) What trends can be identified across programs?

Because access to programmatic information was limited, I developed a questionnaire to obtain more information (see Appendix B). I selected a representative sampling of major and minor programs across the country and wrote to a total of ninety-three programs for information, forty-seven of which responded. A questionnaire was sent to the director of each program to obtain information about the programs not readily accessible in the literature. Thirty-four questionnaires were returned. A combination of the information gathered from the literature review, brochures and syllabi sent by programs, and the questionnaire comprise the foundation of the description of representative programs. I will not present a detailed analysis of my survey responses as the numbers are statistically insignificant.

As we will see, the liberal model predominant in the literature is reflected in the programs. Most peace studies programs can be identified as liberal; that is, they value open, two-way communication, rational dialogue, and the scientific method. They are not looking for revolution, personal or political, but instead, aim for gradual change within the existing structures of society. For the most part, the liberal peace studies programs reflect the institutions that harbor them, and hence, pose no threat to the status quo. Some programs begin to approach the liberationist and transformationist positions in certain aspects, but in general, the vast majority of programs are secured in the liberal tradition.

Before looking at detailed examples of representative programs, I will present some general statistics on peace studies programs to give a general picture of the field. As mentioned earlier, the history of peace studies is not yet a long one. Many of the earliest programs sprang from schools affiliated with Historic Peace Churches, such as the Mennonites, Brethren, and Quakers. Approximately 39.08 percent of peace studies programs, roughly four out of ten, are at religiously affiliated schools (Cianto 1990, 78). Since the mission statements of most of these schools support the teaching and promotion of peace and justice, it is not surprising that the percentage of religiously affiliated peace studies programs is so high. Over half the religiously affiliated programs are affiliated with the Catholic Church, with the next highest representation being Quaker. These early programs often focused on "the role of law in world affairs, and on the peacekeeping potential of the United Nations" (Thomas 1987, 8). The first program was started in 1948 at Manchester College and the next program was not instituted for another eight years.

Many peace studies programs in American universities and colleges were instituted in the early seventies in response to the Civil Rights movement and the Vietnam War, among other things. These programs expanded their studies to include structural violence, such as poverty and oppression. Many more programs sprang up in the 1980s in an attempt to deal with the threat of nuclear war and the challenge of peaceful resolution of conflict. According to COPRED, 117 peace studies programs were created in the United States between 1986 and 1990. More specifically, while COPRED was able to find only 18 full or partial graduate peace studies programs in 1986, they were able to count 39 full and 25 partial graduate programs in 1990 (Cianto 1990, iii). The increase in graduate programs is especially hopeful, signaling expanding interest in research and pursued professions in the field.

In my survey, I attempted to understand how the peace studies programs themselves understood the concept of peace. What does it mean to them? How are they defining peace? This is the most difficult aspect of peace studies to get a handle on, and was, to me, the most important question on the questionnaire because how they view the term "peace" is the basis for all the teaching, programming, and so on, that takes place. The categories chosen for responses to this question are a reflection of the main areas of concern found in the literature and programs of peace studies. I compiled the responses to this question on a graph (see Appendix C) that shows the emphasis or focus of peace studies as perceived by the respondent schools.

Figure 3 shows at a glance the distribution of peace studies programs in the U.S. Each state is shaded according to concentration of programs, black being the heaviest concentration of programs and white being no programs; the actual number of programs is also listed for each state. These programs include graduate and undergraduate degree and non-degree granting programs. The statistics for this figure came from the *Directory of Peace Studies Programs* (Cianto 1990, 73-77).

Through the program analysis, five major foci of university peace studies programs emerged. I identify them as: 1. International Education, World/Global Studies; 2. Conflict Resolution; 3. Nuclear Issues; 4. Spiritual Base; and 5. "Broad-based" (which is particularly eclectic). I will offer one example of each of the first four categories, while I will explore the broad-based approach through several examples. I also will look at some examples of non-degree granting and related programs, which are numerous. An expanded list of examples of representative programs in each category I discuss can be found in Figure 4.

There is no easy way in which to summarize all the distinctive qualities of each peace studies program. In fact, attempting to cover all the programs in some thorough manner would be a book unto itself (e.g., *A Directory of Peace Studies Programs*, Cianto, 1990). (For further examples and a discussion of various peace studies programs, see Lundstrom, D. 1991. An Analysis of Philosophical and Political Foundations of Peace Studies Programs in the United States:

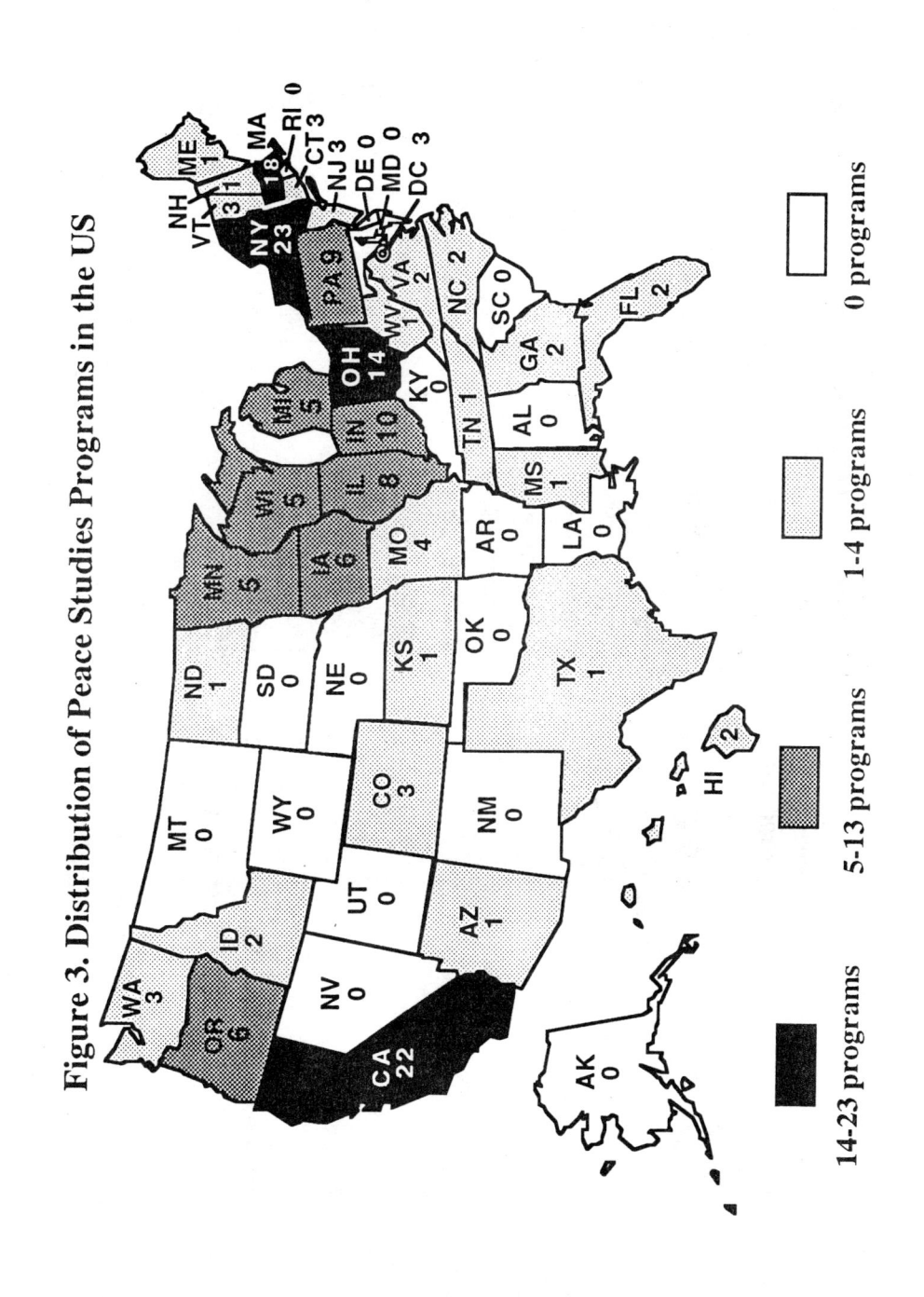

Figure 3. Distribution of Peace Studies Programs in the US

Figure 4. Examples of Representative Peace Studies Programs

	Graduate	Major	Minor
Broad-Based Private	Cal Inst. for Integral Studies Immaculate Heart College Center Incarnate Word College Notre Dame	Bethel College Bluffton College Colgate University Earlham College Juniata College Manchester College Manhattan College Wellesley College Whitworth College William Penn College	Alma College Barry University Bethel College Boston College Chapman College Elizabethtown College Fordham University Iona College Loyola Marymount University Northland College Wilmington College
Broad-Based Public	State Univ. of NY-Binghamton University of Hawaii	University of CA-Berkeley Cal. State Univ.-Sacramento Kent State Univ. of Missouri-Columbia	Univ. of California-Davis Cal. State University-Fresno Florida State University University of Oregon

—continued—

	Graduate	Major	Minor
Broad-Based Public Continued		University of North Dakota Oregon State University Wayne State University Wright State University	Salem State College San Francisco State University So. IL Univ.-Edwardsville Univ. of Wisconsin-Milwaukee
Int'l. Ed.–World–Global Studies	Bowling Green State University University of Colorado-Boulder George Mason University Harvard Law School Univ. of Massachusetts-Boston Univ. of Missouri-St. Louis University of Pennsylvania Pepperdine University Syracuse University Willamette Univ. School of Law	University of Colorado-Boulder John Jay Coll. Criminal Justice Syracuse University	Westchester University

—continued—

	Graduate	Major	Minor
Nuclear Issues	Columbia University Mass. Inst. of Technology (MIT)	University of Washington	Brandeis University University of California-Irvine
Spiritual Base	Assoc. Mennonite Biblical Sem. Earlham College of Religion Iliff School of Theology Seattle University	Georgetown University Molloy College	Briar Cliff College Bridgewater College Calumet College of St. Joseph Carlow College Christian Brothers College College of St. Thomas George Fox College

Toward a Transformative Perspective. M.S.Ed. diss., Department of Leadership and Educational Policy Studies, Northern Illinois University.)

International Education/World-Global Studies

This emphasis in peace studies moves education into the global arena in an attempt to study the world's cultural pluralism and its interrelated systems and problems. These programs focus on understanding the political, economic, and social issues that cut across boundaries. Major topics of interest include world organizations and communities, multicultural education and cultural pluralism. The areas in International Education/World-Global Studies that begin to depart from the liberal model are the imaging/futurism emphasis exemplified by Elise Boulding and the transformationist view of education espoused by Betty Reardon. Both new developments fall into the transformationist category discussed in the last chapter, and do not yet have sufficient emphasis to uproot the International Education/World-Global Studies approach from its liberal base.

Teachers College, Columbia University

Columbia University Teachers College is a private institution in New York. Their graduate Peace Education Program offers a M.S.Ed. or Ed.D. with a concentration in Peace Education. The concentration "is taken in conjunction with specializations in various other masters and doctoral degree programs" (Cianto 1990, 53). The program is housed in The Program in Comparative and International Education.

A minimum of twelve course points are required for the Master's degree, thirty for the Doctorate. In addition to those required by the candidate's major field, courses are chosen from a wide variety of offerings designated as relevant to peace education. Candidates are required to participate for at least one semester in the core peace education seminar, "Education for Peace, Disarmament, and the Control of Nuclear Weapons." The three other required courses are: "Human and Social Dimensions of Peace" (two semesters), "Fundamental Concepts in Peace Education," and "The United Nations as Peace Education." Other electives the student may choose from include: "Education and Freedom," "Psychology of Conflict Resolution," "Political Anthropology: Labor, Race, and Belief," "Seminar in Comparative Human Rights," "Peace Studies (Christian Ethics)," "Theology of Peace: An Ecumenical Perspective," "Educating for Peace and Justice," and "The Politics of Compassion." A major essay is also required for the Master's degree displaying competence in selected issues in the field. For the Doctorate, the certification examination must be supplemented with one in peace education or by an essay equivalent to that at the Master's level. The dissertation must focus on a topic within the realm of, or with relevance to, peace education.

The Director, Betty Reardon, states the purpose of the program: "In recognition of the unprecedented dimensions and overriding significance of problems of war and peace in the nuclear age, Teachers College has developed its Peace Education Program. . . . It is designed to facilitate interdisciplinary study of the educational aspects of the problems of world peace, the arms race, nuclear weapons, problems of social justice, development, human rights, and such related global issues." They also take the study of peace beyond the classroom. "The program also offers internships, research opportunities, various short courses and institutes in association with other organizations and institutions specializing in the fields of peace research and peace education in the United States and other countries. Especially significant among these is the International Institute on Peace Education offered annually during the summer term."

Conflict Resolution

As I discussed in Chapter 2, the Conflict Resolution approach strongly exemplifies peace studies' attempt to integrate the scientific method into the field. This approach is pragmatic and is based on rational theory and control. It relies on open communication, reasonable participation, and is problem-focused. The Conflict Resolution approach is deeply rooted in the liberal tradition and is widely accepted in the field. Yet, as exemplified by the program described below, conflict resolution can begin to move into the transformationist realm with a strong focus on nonviolence.

Syracuse University

Syracuse University (Syracuse, New York) is a private institution of approximately 11,000 undergraduate and 4,000 graduate students. Syracuse's peace studies program is a good example of a program dedicated specifically to the study of conflict. The Program in Nonviolent Conflict and Change (PNCC) began in 1970. The PNCC is both undergraduate and graduate, and grants the degrees B.A. or B.S., and Ph.D. (with a concentration in Conflict Resolution). The PNCC is part of the Maxwell School of Citizenship and Public Affairs, the social sciences division of Syracuse University. Students in the PNCC also work closely with the Program on the Analysis and Resolution of Conflict (PARC). The stated purpose of the PNCC is: "to study creative, peaceful ways of dealing with conflict . . . to develop and expand peace education and research on nonviolent means of resolving conflicts and bringing about or resisting change."

Undergraduate degree requirements include: completion of six core courses, and a minimum of five additional courses in related disciplines such as public affairs, sociology, political science, and history. The six core courses are: (1) Nonviolent action and social change, (2) Nonviolent change in America, (3) Nonviolent action—What it is and how it works, (4) Nonviolent conflict intervention, (5) America in the sixties, and (6) Senior research seminar. Each course of study is planned according to the interests of the student, in consultation with the director of the program. Their brochure states: "The basis of these efforts is an examination of the theory, history, and dynamics of nonviolent movements and techniques, including inquiry into their social-psychological and political dimensions." The faculty background consists of public affairs, sociology, geography, political science, education, psychology, Afro-American studies, and foreign studies.

The PNCC acts as a resource on peace and conflict issues for the greater Syracuse area. From the brochure, we find that the PNCC "conducted training workshops for a variety of groups, organized film series on peace and justice issues, assisted teachers with curriculum development, and led discussions about nonviolence and conflict resolution with community organizations." The PNCC has also sponsored colloquia with such guest speakers as Betty Reardon, Johan Galtung, Elise Boulding, Karl Deutsch, Gene Sharp, George Lakey, and Nigel Young. The director of the PNCC is Neil Katz, renowned scholar in the area of conflict resolution.

Closely related to the PNCC is PARC, the Program on the Analysis and Resolution of Conflicts. This is a non-degree granting program designed "to develop theories that explore the context and stages of different conflicts and to assess and teach alternative methods of conflict resolution . . . PARC activities include theory building seminars, research projects by faculty and students, speaker series, working groups, conferences and seminars. PARC co-sponsors peace studies with Cornell and Colgate University . . ." (Cianto 1990, 63).

PARC grants a Certificate of Achievement in Conflict Analysis and Resolution, and a Certificate of Achievement in Peace Studies in conjunction with graduate degrees in Social Sciences, International Relations, Sociology, Political Science, and other disciplines. An internship is required for the certificate. Graduate students can pursue their interest in conflict resolution and peace studies at Syracuse by designing their own course of study through the interdisciplinary Social Science Program.

Nuclear Issues

As I briefly mentioned in the Chapter 2, the Nuclear Issues approach lies on the conservative end of the liberal spectrum of peace studies. It is deeply rooted in the international relations approach used in early peace studies, and its research is generally focused on scientific methods of quantitative problem-solving.

MIT

The Massachusetts Institute of Technology in Cambridge, Massachusetts offers the MIT Defense and Arms

Control Studies Program (DACS) through their Center for International Studies. DACS is a graduate program and as of 1990, had about thirty Ph.D. candidates in training. DACS is a graduate-level research and teaching activity in security studies and is closely affiliated with the Political Science department. DACS "focuses primarily on military strategy, national security policy, and weaponry, but students can concentrate their work on arms control and alternative methods of international security. The program is known especially for its emphasis on the role of technology in security affairs" (Thomas 1987, 31).

From its information sheet, we learn that "DACS offers a dozen courses on national security topics including trends in defense technologies, comparative strategies, American defense policy and politics, nuclear and conventional arms control policies, comparative defense management, nuclear and conventional force analyses, and the use of military force in international relations."

Extracurricular activities for DACS include sponsoring a general and technical seminar series; conferences (topics include prospects for test ban expansion and the proliferation of nuclear-powered submarines in the Third World); several research working groups (studying areas such as security and economic issues in the North Pacific, conventional forces, Soviet security policies, and current American Defense politics); and several publications, most notably *Soviet Defense Notes*. DACS also provides opportunities for post-doctoral fellows and visitors to work at MIT on security-related projects.

Faculty background for DACS includes: Public Policy and Organization; Defense and Arms Control Studies; Political Science; Science, Technology and National Security Policy; and Electrical Engineering. It is interesting that this program does not appear in COPRED's 1990 compilation of peace studies programs, though it did appear in Thomas's 1987 work. Perhaps the general understanding of what constitutes a peace studies program is narrowing and no longer includes programs that are overwhelmingly focused on negative peace.

Spiritual Base

Though most spiritually based programs remain in the liberal tradition, some begin to take on liberationist and transformationist concerns. The liberationist perspective is present in liberation theologies that are sometimes included in spiritually based programs. As discussed in Chapters 2 and 3, this perspective focuses on the structural violence of inhumane institutions and empowerment of the individual. They sometimes incorporate the transformationist approach through emphasis on personal nonviolence and personal mystical or spiritual journeys as ways to peace. Yet, most of the spiritually based peace studies programs remain well within the liberal tradition and norms.

Associated Mennonite Biblical Seminaries (AMBS)

Associated Mennonite Biblical Seminaries, in Elkhart, Indiana, represents a peace studies program that is strongly based in a Christian theological context.

> The program seeks to integrate the historic peace concern of Mennonites with the emerging Peace Studies discipline. It consists of strong biblical, church historical and theological components which set it apart from secular Peace Studies Programs . . . attention [is] given to expe-

riential learning, contemporary social ethics and the contribution of the social sciences to peace/justice making. Such courses include "Mission-Peace Issues," "Conflict, Communication, Conciliation," and "Peace Colloquium" (Cianto 1990, 50).

AMBS has offered an M.A. in Peace Studies since 1971, and a M.Div. in Peace Studies since 1981. From 1973-1987, more than sixty people have received the M.A. in Peace Studies. Degree requirements include four foundational courses, seven core Peace Studies courses, four additional courses, or two additional courses plus a thesis in Peace Studies. The stated purpose of the program is "How does God's reconciling work in Jesus Christ find expression through the witness of the Christian community in the world? . . . We seek to relate the biblical vision of *shalom* and *mishpat* (peace and justice) to present-day life and issues." The faculty background represents the theological context: Pastoral Care, History, Ethics, Old Testament, Theology, New Testament, and Christian Education. Beyond the classroom, AMBS sponsors guest speakers and local community programs.

Broad-based Programs

Broad-based programs, whether in private or public institutions, include aspects of many or all of the approaches I have discussed thus far. They are inherently eclectic and inclusive.

Manchester College

Manchester College, in North Manchester, Indiana, began its Peace Studies Institute and Program for Conflict

Resolution in 1948. It is a private college affiliated with the Church of the Brethren.

> The Manchester program . . . draws from political science, sociology, psychology, economics, philosophy, and religion. Major attention is given to questions of values and personal relevance as well as historical perspective, conflict resolution, political theory and social change. . . . Most students gain experience through an internship [and] almost every major participates in either a January interim travel/study course or a full one year's study with Brethren Colleges Abroad . . . (Manchester Peace Studies Program Brochure).

Theoretical understanding gained in the classroom is then tested in an active or practical setting.

The undergraduate program grants a B.A., B.S., A.A., and a minor in peace studies. The program is interdisciplinary and requires 43 hours for the major, to include the following distribution of courses: two humanities, three social science, two religion, one philosophy, one economics, one political science, and 12 hours of electives to be approved by the peace studies instructional subcommittee. Required courses are: "Current Issues in Peace and Justice," "Human Conflict," "Conflict Resolution," "Analysis of War and Peace," "Christian Peace Heritage," "Religions and War," "Literature of Nonviolence," "Philosophy of Civilization," "International Economics," and a choice of either "International Politics," or "International Law & Organization." The minor requires 27 hours, including two courses in humanities, one in religion, three in social science, and 9 hours of electives.

Beyond the classroom setting, the Peace Studies Institute sponsors public conferences, programs, concerts and workshops on topics related to conflict resolution. The Institute also publishes the *Bulletin of the Peace Studies Institute and Program in Conflict Resolution*. A number of endowed scholarships are designated for majors and students can take advantage of the Funderburg Library and the peace studies reading room, containing journals and special collections on peace and nonviolence (Cianto 1990, 21).

Notre Dame

The University of Notre Dame, a private, Roman Catholic institution in Notre Dame, Indiana, houses an Institute for International Peace Studies, whose goals are: "to offer a wide array of academic programs at the graduate and undergraduate levels in all five colleges of the University; to develop among the faculty an interest and proficiency in teaching peace courses; to sponsor scholarly research and writing in these areas; and to provide an array of programs for the benefit of the university community and general public" (Cianto 1990, 60). Notre Dame offers an M.A., a Ph.D., and a concentration in peace studies to supplement an undergraduate major.

Master's students choose to concentrate in one of four areas: (1) international peace and world order; (2) cultural, philosophical and religious dimensions of peace and justice; (3) conflict resolution and dispute settlements; or (4) social change for peace, justice, and human rights. M.A. candidates must complete 30 hours (6 of which may be work on a thesis), show proficiency in one foreign language, and pass a comprehensive exam. Doctoral Students, through cooperative arrangements with various Ph.D. programs in the College of Arts & Letters, can "qualify for special Institute fellowships, engage faculty fellows as dissertation directors and participate in the research and teaching activities of the Institute" (Cianto 1990, 60). The undergraduate concentration requires 15 hours of multidisciplinary coursework designed to supplement "one's major field of study with peace, justice, and human rights" (Cianto 1990, 25).

Of national renown is the International Scholars Program, which brings together students from across the globe "to live and study topics on reducing conflict and eliminating human injustices" (Cianto 1990, 60). At any given time, anywhere from a dozen to two dozen or more countries may be represented in the Program. This program directly helps in the broadening of perspectives and understanding of different cultures essential to the creation of peace.

Faculty at Notre Dame's Institute, consisting of thirty-three part-time fellows from fifteen disciplines, also are actively involved. A Faculty and Course Development Workshop is offered each summer to address "how the key questions, concepts and findings of peace research can be incorporated into new and existing courses at the university" (Cianto 1990, 60). Other co-curricular activities at Notre Dame include:

> The Scholarship and Policy Research Programs emphasize the study of international relations in order to establish the Institute as a center for empirical analysis of the values and consequences of state behavior. The Outreach Program sponsors noteworthy speakers on key issues, holds conferences and seminars, and produces videotapes to make campus events available to a wider audience.... Efforts are currently under way to launch a new visiting Fellow's program which will bring scholars and practitioners in the field to the Institute on a short term basis to write, lecture, and research (Cianto 1990, 60).

Overall, clearly Notre Dame has one of the most extensive, well-rounded programs in peace studies in the country. It places strong emphasis on research, yet addresses an active pursuit of peaceful relations through its International Scholars Program. It is pursuing many co-curricular activities, while also devoting time and thought to development of courses and curriculum.

University of Hawaii

The University of Hawaii is a state school located on the island of Honolulu and housing the Institute for Peace. Johan Galtung is Professor of Peace Studies at the University. The program, encompasses both graduate studies and an undergraduate concentration to complement a major. The Institute for Peace is governed by the University Council, which consists of forty faculty members representing more than twenty programs and departments. Fourteen courses are currently offered, most at the graduate level. The program is described as:

> a professionally-oriented one designed to train hands-on professionals. The focus will be on real problems, not academic fields of study. Analytic and experiential work will be blended, with an emphasis placed on building skills of policy analysis, research, conflict management, advocacy, negotiation, and leadership development. Close attention will be paid to the ethical dimensions of formulating public policy issues, and the achievement of peace with peaceful means. The first semester will emphasize problem description; the second semester will focus on problem remedy. Students will choose one of four specializations corresponding to four major values of concern in peace work—peace with security, peace with economic justice, peace with freedom and peace culture—that in addition incorporate ecological concerns. For their third semester, students obtain professional internships, most likely away from Hawaii, and finish the first semester of thesis research. Upon returning for the last semester and finishing thesis research,

students take the Consulting Workshop. Students will regularly interact with faculty, inside and outside of the classroom (Cianto 1990, 55).

The Institute puts a special focus on the Asia-Pacific region, and "is involved with projects such as the Asia-Pacific Dialogue, the South Pacific Human Rights Commission and the Center for Nonviolence" (Cianto 1990, 55). General goals of the Institute are to: "coordinate and stimulate research and education on topics such as the nature and conditions of just and sustainable social order; the relationship between justice, human needs and violence; the causes and conditions of violence, and the paths and struggles leading toward mediation and the resolution of conflict" (Cianto 1990, 55). The University also has a Program on Conflict Resolution, focusing on cross-cultural conflict, which maintains ties with the community conflict resolution center and the courts.

Non-Degree Granting Efforts

There are as many efforts in peace studies that are non-degree granting as there are degree-granting. These efforts vary widely and can be found at the undergraduate and graduate levels in all types of institutions. The basic forms these efforts take are: a few courses or seminars offered; a program still in the planning stages; an Institute or Center for conflict resolution, global education, international cooperation, etc., a peace resource center or library; and support for teaching and research in the field. One school, Norwich University, even has a Peace Corps Preparatory Program. Just to get a sampling, I will look at two peace studies efforts that are non-degree granting.

University of Colorado at Boulder

While the University of Colorado at Boulder does allow students to design an undergraduate peace studies major, of particular interest is their International and National Voluntary Service Training (INVST) Program, designed as a "16 credit hour certification curriculum, available to all undergraduate majors in the University. Students receiving two-year scholarships will fulfill a two-year commitment of community, national, or international service. Two summer sessions are required: the first in the United States and the second abroad" (Cianto 1990, 11).

From the announcement about the program, we learn the purpose of the INVST Program is: "to train students in the study and practice of how peace and justice are achieved and sustained through non-violence. . . . When accepted into the program students will be awarded a scholarship for their Junior and Senior years, in return for which they will serve two years of community, national, or international humanitarian service." Again, from the announcement, the INVST Program is a 17 hour program "centered on 4 courses: Global Human Ecology, Global Development, Facilitating Peaceful Community Change, and Nonviolent Social Movements. Together with each course, students will take a one-unit lab/practicum which affords the practical application of the course content in a community situation. In addition, students will take a one-unit Telecommunications Skills course for developing knowledge in computer networking." The INVST Program offers a wide variety of practical and applied experiences.

New York Metropolitan Peace Studies Consortium

The New York Metropolitan Peace Studies Consortium Project is not a peace studies program, but an attempt to put together graduate courses related to peace studies at universities and colleges in New York and the surrounding vicinity. One of their goals is to create a cooperative doctoral program in Peace Studies. The Project consists of faculty and staff from the New York Metropolitan Area universities and colleges; leaders of private/nonprofit organizations; professionals with the United Nations; and business, government, and professional people with international responsibilities and interests. Aims of the Peace Studies Consortium Project include "the sponsorship of colloquia relevant to the conditions and institutions for peace; a peace studies resource center; increasing the availability of institutional libraries to Peace Studies researchers and the creation of a cooperative program offering a doctorate in Peace Studies or a concentration in Peace Studies in existing doctoral programs." The Consortium published *Peace Studies in Graduate Education*, a reference guide of peace studies courses in the New York Metropolitan Area.

The guide lists and briefly describes some 500 graduate courses dealing with the "broad" subject of peace taught at 19 universities and colleges in the New York Metropolitan area. In an effort to include anything remotely "peaceish" in their guide, the Consortium included almost any course. This over-inclusivity strips peace studies as a field of any focus or clarity, and renders it indistinguishable.

The reference guide lists some classes that can clearly be labeled "peace studies," such as: "Critical Thinking for Peace Studies," "Psychology of Conflict Resolution and Justice," and "Peace in the American Tradition." However, in an attempt to list any and everything that may even remotely carry a seed of being related to peace studies, the Reference Guide also includes the following courses: "Economic Organization and Development of Japan," "International Marketing," "International Banking," "International Accounting," "The Expansion of Europe, 1200-1700," and "International Corporate Financing." Course descriptions include: "Case analyses of evolving competitive relationships among banks in an international environment," "Strategic business practices to maximize corporate opportunities," and "Explanations of current difficulties in international monetary relations between advanced capitalist countries. . . . No consideration of developing countries' problems apart from debt problem."

One can readily see the problem that arises. Any course that has the word "comparative," "international," or "global" in its title automatically qualifies as peace studies. Any course in which one learns anything about other countries, including how to better exploit them, is called peace studies. The obvious problem is that being global or international is in no way a sufficient condition for a course being classified as peace studies. On the other hand, almost any subject matter, taught in the right way and with the proper focus, has the potential of becoming a peace studies class. We must limit the courses we label as "peace studies" if we are to maintain it as a distinguishable field.

Through the statistics at the beginning of this chapter, I presented a general description of the field of peace studies programs in the U.S. As Figure 3 revealed, the largest representations of programs are found in New York and California. The most consistent clusterings are seen on the East and West coasts and in the Great Lakes region. Nearly 40 percent of these programs are religiously affiliated, with 55 percent of religiously affiliated programs being Roman Catholic. Five main categories surfaced through the research and I discussed each through representative programs.

The **International Education/World-Global Studies** approach focuses on the future and the ability to imagine alternate world futures in order to create peace. It aims at transforming relationships on a personal as well as an international level and believes that open and inclusive education about cultural differences is necessary to create a more peaceful world. Increased understanding of other cultures and perspectives are important aspects of this approach. Exposing students to many different cultures and viewpoints is paramount, with the goal being better understanding of world pluralism and world systems. Its premise is that peace requires understanding; therefore, if there is ever to be world peace, we must understand the world's cultural pluralism. International and cross-cultural internships and other co-curricular opportunities are emphasized to reach this goal. Courses in Non-Western or Comparative Culture, Global Studies, and Foreign Languages are stressed. Though it at times steps into the realm of transformationism, this approach is for the most part solidly liberal.

The **Conflict Resolution** approach focuses on transforming violent or potentially violent conflicts into nonviolent resolutions at the personal, interpersonal, societal, national, and international levels. In the classroom, students study creative, peaceful ways of dealing with conflict. Often, the basis of this approach is an examination of the theory, history, and dynamics of nonviolent movements and techniques, including inquiry into their social-psychological and political dimensions. Faculty from many areas teach conflict resolution; however, new specialists in the field are becoming more prominent as teachers. The conflict resolution approach stresses simulation more than any other of the approaches, and for obvious reasons. If one is to become a successful conflict mediator, one must practice mediating conflicts. Internships and other experiences resolving conflicts outside the classroom are of great importance. Conflict Resolution is pragmatic, and is strongly rooted in the liberal tradition of rational, problem-centered study.

The **Nuclear Issues** approach is closely tied to the methods and subject matter of political science and international relations. Since it focuses on nuclear weapons and the possibility of nuclear war, it is highly concerned with foreign policy, strategic studies, the military, defense, and security. The main topics of study in this approach are defense and the role of nuclear weapons in defense. Students are prepared to become experts in the analysis and creation of policies of defense, national security, and arms control. Many end up working for the government, U.S. or otherwise. The Nuclear Issues approach represents the most conservative trend in peace studies. Like Conflict Studies, it is rooted in the liberal tradition of scientific problem solving.

Spiritually-based programs obviously come from the ideological base of a particular religion. The major religions preach love, peace, and justice, and consequently provide a natural base for peace studies. All the religiously affiliated peace studies programs in the U.S. come from a Christian base. Therefore, the underlying beliefs of these programs center on one's proper relationship to God and living and spreading his message. These peace studies programs have strong biblical, church historical and theological components that set them apart from secular programs. "Most of these religion-based programs . . . offer a curriculum combining church teachings on peace and justice, a commitment to social activism, and an emphasis on the relevance of inter-personal behavior to relations between groups and societies" (Thomas

1987, 19). While strongly rooted in the liberal tradition, Spiritually Based programs at times take on a liberationist or transformationist approach.

Broad-based programs include aspects of all the approaches discussed above. They are truly inclusive. Of course, in taking this approach, one is not able to cover a topic as thoroughly or extensively as in the more focused approaches. For instance, in the conflict resolution approach, a student may take three or four classes in conflict resolution and participate in several simulations and an internship in conflict resolution; whereas, in a broad-based program, the student may only take one course in, or simply touch on, conflict resolution in another course. There are obvious advantages and disadvantages to both. However, peace itself is a widely inclusive term, and this approach reflects that inclusive nature. Though most Broad-based programs remain in the liberal perspective, a few begin to break out into incorporating liberationist and transformationist concerns. To some degree, all the approaches to peace studies previously discussed are broad-based. None of the approaches is disciplinary; all are transdisciplinary and encompass different fields and methodologies. What do all of these approaches have in common?

Most basically, all approaches value and are trying to bring about peace. And as I just mentioned, all peace studies programs are transdisciplinary, reflecting the complexity of the subject matter. We find programs in the World/Global Issues approach studying arms control; those in the Nuclear Issues approach studying conflict negotiation; those in Conflict Management studying nonviolence and justice. And blanketing most of the approaches is the study of the history, methods, and dynamics of nonviolence. Each method or approach wants to change or transform current relationships, making them more peaceful, cooperative, and loving; therefore, all the programs focus, to some degree, on the future. Also, all of these approaches emphasize imagination, creativity, and the broadening of possibilities to some degree.

Almost all the programs come from a liberal perspective. They try to bring about peace through gradual change in the existing nation-state system. They are not looking to overthrow institutions or to reconstruct the state, but in contrast, they search for reform. This limits their capacity to imagine and launch counter suggestions to war in threatening situations. They are largely positivistic, retaining ties to the international relations approach. The scientific method is highly valued; consequently, much research is concerned with prediction and control of violent conflict. Classrooms are democratic with the teacher and students working together in an atmosphere of cooperation and rational inquiry. They are problem-centered and focus on the individual. Open communication and critical thinking skills are highly valued. Students are taught to question intelligently and thoroughly all that is presented. Most peace studies programs hope to produce critically aware citizens who are prepared to work in a democratic society in an informed and intelligent way.

Where the programs differ is obvious. Some interpret peace as the absence of war and armed conflict, some as personal, inner peace, some as resolving conflicts nonviolently. The varying interpretations are revealed in the varying types of programs. Some focus on creation and maintenance of a level of negative peace, while others strive for total world peace and justice. All ultimately are working for the same thing, just at various levels and stages, from different angles.

I have argued that the most powerful and promising of the ideologies found in peace studies is transformationism. As we have discovered, most peace studies programs today are rooted in the liberal approach, and are having a limited impact. What are the curricular implications of transformationism? If one could create an ideal peace studies program from a transformationist perspective, what would it look like? How might it differ from the examples we have seen?

6. Curricular Implications of the Transformationist Approach

I have described and analyzed the main ideologies found in peace studies, and explored the philosophical underpinnings of the various types of peace studies programs that exist in this country. Ultimately what we need for the creation of peace is simultaneous self, communal, and societal improvement; transcendence of the nation-state perspective; and serious study, development, and practice of the philosophy of nonviolence. The transformationist approach addresses all of these concerns.

As we have discovered, the values and goals of transformationism reflect the shift to a new paradigm. Realization of ultimate oneness, of interconnectedness and consequent interdependency is the basis of, the common connection between, all of the new paradigm concerns. It is the foundational belief of transformationist peace education. Transformationist peace education and the new paradigm present us with a belief system, a set of ideas, that is balanced, holistic, healthy, and completely integrated. They do not throw out the old paradigm and reductionistic thought, they simply balance the scales by adding emergent properties and downward causation to the scientific process. The reductionistic process of microdeterminism is complemented by the emergent process of macrodeterminism. The old paradigm yang values of assertiveness and competition are complemented by the new paradigm values of responsive, cooperative yin elements. Rationality and analytic thought are balanced by intuition and subjective experience. In fact, the entire evolution from the old paradigm to the new is a great balancing act: adding more yin qualities to tip the scales to an even, healthy level. We should not confuse this process as placing a higher value on feminine, subjective yin characteristics; fixation on either extreme of the continuum is dangerous. Flexibility and movement between the ends of this process is the most important aspect.

The classroom atmosphere for transformationist peace education must itself be democratic, fostering critical and open discussion. It must be active, varied, and participatory, involving each student. The teacher must be a guide, and must treat the students as equals. It should emphasize self-knowledge, critical awareness, and sensitivity. Fear and competition should play no part. Peace education should emphasize freedom and love, preparing students to revolt if they must, even against peace education! How might these ideas translate into a transformationist peace studies program? What areas or subject matter would be critical? What specific classes would be offered, and how would it be structured? If an institution had no restraints financially and had all necessary resources, how would they go about creating an ideal peace studies program?

To begin, a peace studies committee would be formed of interested and dedicated faculty, administrators and students interested in getting the program off the ground. The committee would meet regularly, and for any special decision-making. One person from this group would be chosen chair, and act as special academic advisor for Peace Studies majors. The chair might be someone who is teaching the core course. Others on the committee may want to volunteer as resource persons or to help with publicity for the program.

The first step in starting a program is for the peace studies committee to develop a conceptual map of peace studies (Lopez 1989a, 75). With the help of the map, faculty can decide which areas of focus they can teach. Second, an inventory of participating faculty and institutional resources should be taken to determine strengths and weaknesses. Finally, the intricacies of the program can be worked through, such as internship or other practical experience, the role of the introductory course, and so on. Lastly, "the committee should produce a clear statement of purpose for the program that can be distributed to appropriate campus bodies, including the faculty and administrative entities responsible for academic affairs, the various departments, and the school newspaper" (Lopez 1989a, 79). Gathering of potential written and audio-visual resources is also of great importance. Resource persons on the committee would start files, accumulating journals, articles, book titles, audio-visual aids, and lists of peace and justice organizations and events. These files, then, could be tapped by all faculty teaching in the major, as well as students.

The program would be housed within the interdisciplinary portion of a college. An interdisciplinary rather than a departmentally based major has advantages. While being grounded in a department may help to give the major greater respectability and security, it also risks becoming the "business" of that department. In other words, if the major is interdisciplinary, there will be a greater sense that the University "owns" the program, and all the faculty from various departments are responsible for the success of the program. There will be a greater vested interest if the program is interdisciplinary. More basically, "because violence in the global system (whether military or 'structural') results from a combination of political, economic, social, and cultural factors, any comprehensive analysis of the subject must draw upon the methodologies and the accumulated wisdom of many fields, including history, economics, psychology, anthropology, sociology, and political science" (Klare 1989, 64). Peace studies is naturally interdisciplinary. To avoid parochialism, to study peace in a truly global, world sense, which it must be by its nature, "third world" societies and cultures cannot be neglected. Peace must be approached not only in an interdisciplinary, but an international manner (Galtung 1985, 143). We cannot simply take an American or a Northern European approach to peace; we must look at peace from as many different civilizational perspectives as possible.

Also, the program would be experientially, as well as theoretically, based. An internship would be required. Possibilities include volunteering at a local homeless shelter, working at a shelter for battered or abused women, a soup kitchen, a local chapter of Amnesty International, Greenpeace, or another local peace and justice group. Ideally, students would have a chance to intern internationally with peace and justice groups of other cultures.

Peace studies courses would ideally be taught by women and men of varying cultures and perspectives. Teachers would be guides, with students taking much of the responsibility for teaching and learning, including leading discussions. Classes would be multi-faceted and active, using not only books and other written sources, but films, simulations, small group discussions, role playing, and other multi-media techniques. The classroom would be a place without fear, allowing for open, trust-filled discussion and debate. All opinions would be welcomed. Guest speakers would be brought in to share insights, and students would frequently leave the classroom to learn from other sources, such as the Peace Museum or the Midwest Peace Institute. Students, including the teacher, would keep a journal to create and keep note of their ongoing reflective dialogue of personal peace and related issues, which would help enormously in keeping everyone focused and aware. Grading would be discussed among the group to determine appropriate measures. Once the foundation has been laid, what might the specific curriculum entail?

The ideal major would begin with an introductory course. This would briefly cover the history of the peace movement and nonviolence, an introduction to the concept of peace, and would briefly deal with the issues of nuclear arms, conflict resolution, and various peace and justice issues of the day.

Four core areas crucial to the study of peace in this approach are: conflict resolution, nonviolence, nuclear issues, and spirituality and peace. These would be the required four subjects areas, each offering three to four courses from which to choose. Specialists in these four areas within their departments would teach these courses. Several electives would be part of the program, and at least one teacher from each of the following departments would be part of the peace studies committee and would teach a peace studies course in her or his specialization once at least every four semesters: anthropology, art, biology, communications, economics, education, English, geography, geology, history, human and family resources, international relations, journalism, music, philosophy, physics, political science, psychology, sociology, technology, theater, and women's studies. Twelve courses would be required for the major. The introductory course would ideally be a prerequisite to the other courses, so that the student gets a broad overview before delving into specific courses. The four other mandatory classes would be chosen from electives in Conflict Management, Nonviolence Theory and Action, The Nuclear Age, and Spiritual and Ethical Perspectives on Peace. At least two of the four mandated elective groups would offer courses each semester. Six other courses would be chosen from seven categories of electives: Artistic, Literary, and Media Perspectives on Peace; Ecological Balance; Human Rights and Social Justice; Militarism, War, and International Conflict; Women and Peace; World Order Education and Alternative Futures; and World Political Economy and Economic Justice. These elective courses would be taught at least once every four semesters.

Major in Peace Studies

Requirements (36)

Core course (3)

    IDSP   ____: Introduction to Peace Studies (3)

Electives from the following: (30)

For the elective courses, no more than 12 semester hours may be applied from any one department. No more than 9 semester hours of elective coursework may be taken in your major.

One course to be taken from each of the following four groups:

Conflict Resolution (3)

    COMS   ____: Communication and Conflict Management (3)
    IDSP   ____: Conflict Resolution and Negotiation (3)

Nonviolence Theory and Action (3)

    HIST   ____: History of Nonviolent Resistance (3)
    PHIL   ____: The Great Philosophers of Nonviolence (3)
    POLS   ____: Techniques, Strategies, and Politics of Nonviolent Action (3)
    SOCI   ____: Nonviolent Social Change (3)

The Nuclear Age (3)

    ANTH   ____: Culture and Nuclear War (3)
    HIST   ____: America in the Nuclear Age (3)
    PHYS   ____: Physics and Society: Nuclear Issues (3)
    TECH   ____: Science, Technology, and Arms Control (3)

Spiritual and Ethical Perspectives on Peace (3)

    IDSP   ___: Being Peace (3)
    PHIL   ___: Contemporary Religious Ethics: War and Peace in a Nuclear Age (3)
    SOCI   ___: Social Ethics (3)

One course to be taken from six of the following seven groups:

Artistic, Literary, and Media Perspectives on Peace

    ART   ___: War and Peace in Art Through the Ages (3)
    ENGL   ___: War and Peace in English and American Literature (3)
    JOUR   ___: The Press and the Arms Race (3)
    MUSC   ___: Music of Protest and Hope (3)
    THEA   ___: Images of War and Peace in Twentieth Century Film (3)

Ecological Balance

    BIOS   ___: Environmental Biology (3)
    GEOG   ___: Natural Resources and Environmental Quality (3)
    GEOL   ___: Environmental Geology (3)
    SOCI   ___: Environmental Sociology (3)
    TECH   ___: Introduction to Appropriate Technology (3)

Human Rights and Social Justice

    ECON   ___: Human Rights and Economic Development (3)
    HFR   ___: Human Rights, Human Dignity, and Human Needs (3)
    ILAS   ___: The U.N. and the Universal Declaration of Human Rights (3)
    POLS   ___: Southern Africa: Race, Class, and Political Change (3)

Militarism, War, and International Conflict

    HIST   ___: The Middle East since 1914 (3)
    POLS   ___: Latin American Politics: Actors, Issues, and Models (3)
    POLS   ___: Third World Revolutions (3)

Women and Peace

ILAS	___:	Feminist Issues and World Peace (3)
ILAS	___:	Women of Peace across Cultures and Centuries (3)
ILAS	___:	Women, Peace, and Protest (3)

World Order Education and Alternative Futures

ENGL	___:	Utopias and Dystopias (3)
EdPSYC	___:	Imaging a Peaceful World (3)
ILAS	___:	International Law and a Just World Order (3)
EDUC	___:	Educating for Peace (3)
EDUC	___:	Foundations of Peace Education (3)

World Political Economy and Economic Justice

ECON	___:	Comparative Economics and International Development (3)
ECON	___:	Economics for Peacemakers (3)
HFR	___:	Global Food and World Nutrition (3)
HIST	___:	The Experience and Legacy of Colonialism (3)
POLI	___:	The State and Third World Development (3)

Internship (3) to be obtained in consultation with the Program Advisor.

Although this curriculum would prove to be a demanding major, it reflects the complexity and vast nature of the study of peace. I created the four mandatory electives from the areas I deemed most important to the transformationist approach. Nonviolence—its history, development, techniques, and strategies—is particularly important to the transformationist approach. Transformationism also singles out the spiritual and ethical dimensions of peace. Each person's spiritual journey plays a fundamental role in the creation of peace. The inclusion of conflict resolution and nuclear issues as mandatory courses may seem surprising coming from a transformationist perspective. But, these two subject areas are of no less concern to transformationist peace educators than they are to other peace educators. The fact remains that a large part of peace studies boils down to resolving conflicts peacefully and nonviolently at various levels. Conflict resolution skills are crucial to any attempt to create peace. Nuclear issues also are of grave importance. The imminent danger of nuclear weapons and the legacy of nuclear energy are the biggest and most threatening creations to date. Therefore, peace studies students must be aware of and knowledgeable about the issues concerning nuclear weapons and energy.

The point of teaching peace studies courses is to make peacemakers out of students. Students will not only gain cognitive knowledge about peace and war issues, but also will come away with other skills, such as: analyzing real-life conflict situations from interpersonal to global levels, resolving conflicts of many sorts, envisioning alternative futures, and possibly leading lives of nonviolence and service. Ultimately, we can attempt to teach being peace, but there are no guarantees. We cannot force another person to be or become peace in their day-to-day lives. All we can do as teachers is expose students, open them up, to examples of being peace. Our best means of conveying being peace is ourselves. We also can use examples through books, journals, films, field trips, simulations, and other practical experiences. The most profound and meaningful part of peace studies is helping another to progress on their spiritual journey. This is an acutely personal adventure. We can point to the path, but we cannot push, or even pull, someone down it.

Peace education makes peace more real. It helps us to imagine, or envision a peaceful world. It helps us to understand and create peace. Ernst Toller suggests the following provocative ideas for teaching peace: Banish the spirit of war from all schools, books, and other media; teach that peace is not a state, but a risk; that peace is a dangerous and adventurous task; that peace is the revolutionary activity of humankind; that a hero's death is a small thing in comparison with a heroic life for great moral aims; teach them to love the adventure of peace (Weinberg 1963, 183-84).

Conclusion

It is crucial today to address the issues of war and peace, not in some perfunctory manner, but in depth and at length. There is no escaping the issue of peace in our time. It is a matter of ultimate importance, it is a matter of survival. With the state of the world, physically, and psychologically, something must be done if we are to continue as a species, along with all other species, and the earth itself. "For that reason alone there would be an extraordinary failure by academics . . . were they not to undertake a systematic study of the conditions of contemporary peace" (O'Connell and Curle 1985, 7).

Universities help to create future leaders. Are we educating students properly about real possibilities for peace? Are we offering them courses in peacemaking skills? Are we helping them to become local, national, and international peace leaders? Do we care enough about making peace a reality to act on creating peace studies programs? Can we afford not to? Now more than ever, we need peacemaking skills and knowledge. Ultimately, the creation of a peace studies program helps a university to fulfill its traditional mission or purpose—to pursue new knowledge, theories, and strategies for bettering the human and social condition (Thomas 1987, 22).

Peace studies is a field of changing realities, still struggling to define itself. It identifies problems, conflicts, wars, tensions, injustices, and then tries to find ways of correcting, alleviating, or eliminating them. "Peace studies is an interdisciplinary academic field that analyzes the causes of war, violence, and systemic oppression, and explores processes by which conflict and change can be managed so as to maximize justice while minimizing violence. It encompasses the study of economic, political, and social systems at the local, national and global levels, and of ideology, culture, and technology as they relate to conflict and change" (Thomas 1987, 5). Peace studies is not some sentimental attempt for everyone to love one another or to make everyone friends. It does not support suppressing dissent; nor does it have as a goal the elimination of conflict. It struggles to make democracy a reality both in society and in the classroom. Some may argue that peace studies does not qualify as a discipline in the traditional sense. But what difference does that make? If the study of peace is carried out "with intellectual rigor, offers new and valid insights and generalizations, and has some practical significance" (O'Connell and Curle 1985, 10), then it is worthy of our time and effort.

Most of the research and teaching efforts in peace studies are grounded in the liberal tradition. Though it is well-intended, this approach to peace education is not having that great of an impact. Because it seeks gradual reform within the existing system, it does not seek to root out and replace the systems of structural violence in our society. Liberalism ultimately preserves the status quo. While liberationism does aim to overthrow the institutions of structural violence and reconstruct the state in a more humane fashion, most liberationist theories emphasize reductionist transformation. Because our problems are not only caused by systemic structural violence but also by the system of thought that created it, we also must work from an emergent viewpoint to transform our thoughts, beliefs, values, and actions on an individual level. Ultimately, ideologies based in materialism, including liberalism and liberationism, are unable to address the full spectrum of human existence. Transformationism provides the necessary inclusivity to take us into the future peacefully.

I examined the systemic crises of patriarchy and capitalism and the conditions these problems produce. The transformationists argue that we cannot wait for inhumane institutions to be replaced to begin to transform ourselves for peace since our distortive collective psyches also created those systems of oppression. We are not separate from institutionalized structural violence. To solve these problems and bring about peace would require efforts not only to transform our institutions, but the system of thought that created them. Therefore, we must simultaneously work at transforming our institutions and our consciousnesses actively to bring about peace.

Working individually at being peace is unique to the transformationist approach to peace studies. It is the key element the liberationist approach lacks. I explored being peace at length through definition and modes of arising, as well as looking at examples of being peace. We saw that life is suffering, much of which is caused by the ego. Through awareness and mindfulness, the ego reveals itself to be illusory, leading to the conclusion that there is no self. This process of discovery leads to the realization that everything is our relation, and that all life is intimately interconnected. This realization often leads to a lifestyle of unconditional love, nonviolence, and service. Such transformation ideally leads to being peace.

Realizing that our problems are not only caused by institutional violence, but also are human caused leaves us with a moral responsibility to work for change. We cannot afford to precipitate the divisiveness of nation, class, race, religion, or gender if we want to survive in peace. This means that if we, as mature adults, care about the world we live in, we have a responsibility to educate ourselves in whatever way we can so that we may proceed intelligently, and, I argue, compassionately, in all areas of our lives. If we truly want world peace, we must work diligently and whole-heartedly at it in our personal lives. We must try to learn and practice being peace in our everyday lives. The theories and practices of transformationist peace education are ready to help us in this process.

The underlying current in the educational process of becoming peace is one of change, of transformation. If we think about it, everything about peace and peace studies points to change: changing our ways of thinking, our relationships, our behaviors, our patterns. There can be no peace without change. Change must take place not only in the relationships of power, control, and democracy, but more fundamentally, they must take place in our thoughts and modes of thinking. In the words of John Stuart Mill, "No great improvements in the lot of [humankind] are possible until a great change takes place in the fundamental constitution of [our] modes of thought."

Transformationist peace education reflects the transition from the one-sided, materialistic paradigm of the past to a new, holistic paradigm. This is a hopeful sign in the development of human beings as a species. Widescale adoption of these ideas would be a great step up on the ladder of consciousness evolution. The future of the emerging form of humanity that the new paradigm, peace education, and our efforts to be peace will help to produce is concretized in John White's vision of "Homo Noeticus." This new person is non-competitive, non-aggressive, benevolent, and ethical.

S/he is cooperative and loving, and has great self-understanding and deep awareness. Noeticus, the study of consciousness, is one of the main concerns of this new breed (White 1988, 123). Though idealistic, this vision provides a role model of how we might be peace and transform our world into one of peace in the future.

Appendices

Appendix A

Peace and/or Peace Studies Journals

The ANNALS of the American Academy of Political and Social Science
Buddhist Peace Fellowship Newsletter
Bulletin of the Atomic Scientists
COPRED Peace Chronicle
Fellowship of Reconciliation Newsletter
The History and Social Science Teacher
International Peace Research Newsletter
International Peace Studies Newsletter
Journal of Conflict Resolution
Journal of Peace Abstracts
Journal of Peace Research
Journal of Social Issues

Peace & Change
Peace and Freedom
Peace News
SIPRI Year Book (Stockholm International Peace Research Institute)

Appendix B

Questionnaire

1. What year was your peace studies program instituted?

2. Is it interdisciplinary, or an emphasis within a department?

3. What is the size of your school?
    - ___ Under 500 students
    - ___ 500-1000
    - ___ 1000-2500
    - ___ 2500-5000
    - ___ 5000-10,000
    - ___ 10,000-15,000
    - ___ 15,000-20,000
    - ___ Over 20,000

4. How many enrolled majors or minors are there in your program?

5. As we know, peace is a complex concept with many nuances, making it difficult to define. What do you feel the main emphasis or focus of "peace" at your school is?
   ___ Conflict Resolution   ___ Spiritual Base
   ___ Justice   ___ Nonviolence
   ___ Nuclear Issues   ___ Global/World Issues
   ___ Transformation/
       empowerment   ___ Other_____

6. Does your program require an internship or other practical experience?

7. What has been your most frustrating experience with peace studies?

8. What has been your most positive, or hopeful experience with peace studies?

9. What, if any, innovations or changes do you encourage or support in teaching style, method, or classroom environment for peace studies classes?

10. How is the level of institutional support for your program?

11. Do you perceive the demand among students for peace studies classes to be rising, falling, or maintaining?

12. What would you like to see as a next step for your program?

Appendix C

Emphasis or Focus of Peace Studies at Respondent Peace Studies Schools

	Global-World Issues	Justice	Conflict Resolution	Non-violence	Nuclear Issues	Spiritual Base	Other*	Transformation/ Empowerment
18								
16	16							
14								
12		12						
10								
8			8					
6				6				
4				4	4	4	4	
2								2
0								

*"Other" includes: Environment/ecological, war/peace issues, interdisciplinary, and various combinations, including "all of the above."

Bibliography

Alger, Chadwick. 1986. The Quest for Peace. *Mershon Center Quarterly Report* (Autumn) 11, no. 2.

———. 1987. A Grassroots Approach to Life in Peace: Self-Determination in Overcoming Peacelessness. *Bulletin of Peace Proposals* 18, no. 3:375-92.

———. 1989. Peace Studies at the Crossroads: Where Else? *The Annals of the American Academy of Political and Social Science* (July) 504:117-27.

Alker Jr., Hayward R. 1988. Emancipatory Empiricism: Toward the Renewal of Empirical Peace Research. In Wallensteen, Peter, ed. *Peace Research: Achievements and Challenges*. Boulder, CO: Westview Press.

Barnaby, Frank, ed. 1988. *The Gaia Peace Atlas*. New York: Doubleday Books.

Bing, Anthony G. 1989. Peace Studies as Experiential Education. *The Annals of the American Academy of Political and Social Science* (July) 504:48-60.

Boucher, Norman. 1972. Peace Research: Dialectics and Development. *Journal of Conflict Resolution,* 16, no. 4:469-75.

———. 1975. New Careers and New Societies: Challenges for College Peace Studies Programs. *Journal of World Education.*

———. 1983. Learning Peace: bills in Congress to found a national peace academy have started a debate over who should teach and study peace. *The Atlantic* (September) 252:12-15.

Boulding, Elise. 1982. Education for Peace. *Bulletin of the Atomic Scientists* (June) 38:59-62.

———. 1987. Learning Peace. In Hanrieder, Wolfram F., ed. *Global Peace and Security: Trends and Challenges.* Boulder, CO: Westview Press.

———. 1988. Image and Action in Peace Building. *Journal of Social Issues,* 44, no. 2:17-37.

Boulding, Kenneth. 1978. *Stable Peace.* Austin: University of Texas Press.

Bowles, Samuel, and Herbert Gintis. 1983. *Schooling in Capitalist America.* In O'Neill, William F. *Rethinking Education: Selected Readings in the Educational Ideologies.* Dubuque, IA: Kendall/Hunt.

Brock-Utne, Birgit. 1985. *Educating for Peace: A Feminist Perspective.* New York: Pergamon Press.

———. 1987. The Relationship of Feminism to Peace and Peace Education. In Carson, Terrance R., and Hendrik D. Gideonse, eds. *Peace Education and the Task for Peace Educators.* A World Council for Curriculum and Instruction Monograph.

———. 1989. *Feminist Perspectives on Peace and Peace Education.* New York: Pergamon Press.

Brown, Peggy, ed. 1983. Peace Studies. *Forum for Liberal Education* (March) 5, no. 4.

Bryan, Dale A. 1989. Internship Education in Peace and Justice Studies: The Tufts University Experience. In Thomas Daniel C., and Michael T. Klare, eds. *Peace and World Order Studies: A Curriculum Guide.* 5th ed. Boulder, CO: Westview Press.

Burns, Robin. 1981. Development Education and Peace Education: From Conflict to Cooperation. *United Nations Development Education Paper* no. 22, UNICEF.

Burns, Robin. 1987. Peace Education and Curriculum. In Carson, Terrance R., and Hendrik D. Gideonse, eds. *Peace Education and the Task for Peace Educators*. A World Council for Curriculum and Instruction Monograph.

Byron, S.J., and William J. 1988. Peace Studies Should Be Taught as 'the History and Management of Conflict Resolution.' *The Chronicle of Higher Education* (23 November).

Cady, Duane. 1989. *From Warism to Pacifism: A Moral Continuum*. Philadelphia: Temple University Press.

Caplow, Theodore. 1989. *Peace Games*. Middletown, CT: Wesleyan University Press.

Capra, Fritjof. 1982. *The Turning Point*. New York: Bantam Books.

Carey, Dennis. 1980. A Discipline Development Model for Peace Studies. *Peace & Change* 6, no. 1 and 2:90-98.

Carro, Jorge L. 1987. Education for Peace: Education or Indoctrination? *Vital Speeches of the Day* 54, no. 5:157-61.

Carson, Terrance R., and Hendrik D. Gideonse, eds. 1987. *Peace Education and the Task for Peace Educators*. A World Council for Curriculum and Instruction Monograph. New York.

Cianto, David, comp. 1990. *A Directory of Peace Studies Programs*. Fairfax, VA: COPRED.

Chatfield, Charles. 1979. International Peace Research: The Field Defined by Dissemination. *Journal of Peace Research* 16, no. 2:163-79.

_____. ed. 1973. *Peace Movements in America*. New York: Schocken Books.

Clarken, Rodney H. 1986. Achieving Peace Through Education. Paper presented at the 33rd World Assembly of the International Council on Education for Teaching. 20-24 July, Kingston, Jamaica.

_____. 1988. Education for Peace. Paper presented at the World Peace Council and UNESCO International Encounter for Peace, Disarmament, and Life. 19-24 April, Merida, Venezuela.

Cohen, Carl, ed. 1972. *Communism, Fascism, Democracy*. New York: Random House, Inc.

Conetta, Carl, ed. 1988/89. *Peace Resource Book: A Comprehensive Guide to Issues, Groups, and Literature*. Cambridge, MA: Ballinger Publishing Company.

Consortium on Peace Research, Education and Development. 1972. COPRED Questionnaire on Peace Research, Education and Action: A Report, *Peace & Change* 1, no. 1:62-67.

Counts, George S. 1932. *Dare the School Build a New Social Order?* New York: Stratford Press.
Cox, C. and R. Scruton. 1984. *Peace Studies: A Critical Survey.* London: Institute for European Defence and Strategic Studies.
Crews, Robin J. 1989. A Values-Based Approach to Peace Studies. In Thomas, Daniel C., and Michael T. Klare, eds. 1989. *Peace and World Order Studies: A Curriculum Guide.* 5th ed. Boulder, CO: Westview Press.
Curle, Adam. 1974. *The Scope and Dilemmas of Peace Studies.* Bradford: University of Bradford.
Dandavate, Madhu. 1977. *Marx and Gandhi.* Bombay: Popular Prakashan.
Dass, Ram and Paul Gorman. 1987. *How Can I Help?* New York: Alfred A. Knopf, Inc.
DeBenedetti, Charles. 1984. Peace History, in the American Manner. *History-Teacher* (November) 18, no. 1:75-110.
DeBenedetti, Charles, ed. 1986. *Peace Heroes in Twentieth Century America.* Bloomington: Indiana University Press.
Dellinger, David. 1970. *Revolutionary Nonviolence.* New York: Bobbs-Merrill, Co.
Deming, Barbara. 1986. Pacifism. *Peace News* (10 January):10-11.
Dewey, John. 1944. *Democracy and Education.* New York: Macmillin Co.
_____. 1983. My Pedagogic Creed. In O'Neill, William F. *Rethinking Education: Selected Readings in the Educational Ideologies.* Dubuque, IA: Kendall/Hunt.
Educators for Social Responsibility. 1983. *Perspectives: A Teaching Guide to Concepts of Peace.* Cambridge, MA: Educators for Social Responsibility.
Ehrenreich, Barbara. 1989. Life Without Father: Reconsidering Socialist-Feminist Theory. In *An Anthology of Western Marxism*, ed. Roger S. Gottlieb. Oxford: Oxford University Press.
_____. 1990. The Warrior Culture. *Time,* 15 October, p. 100.
Einstein, Albert. 1960. *Einstein on Peace.* New York: Simon & Schuster.
Elshtain, Jean Bethke. 1987. *Women and War.* New York: Basic Books, Inc.
Everts, Philip P. 1972. Developments and Trends in Peace and Conflict Research, 1965-1971: A Survey of Institutions. *Journal of Conflict Resolution,* 16, no. 4:477-510.

Ferguson, Marilyn. 1980. *The Aquarian Conspiracy.* Los Angeles: J. P. Tarcher, Inc.

Fields, Rick, with Peggy Taylor, Rex Weyler, and Rick Ingrasci. 1984. *Chop Wood, Carry Water.* Los Angeles: Jeremy P. Tarcher, Inc.

Fink, Clinton. 1980. Peace Education and the Peace Movement since 1815. *Peace and Change,* vol. 6, no. 1-2.

Fischer, Dietrich, with Wilhelm Nolte and Jan Oberg. 1989. *Winning Peace: Strategies and Ethics for a Nuclear-Free World.* New York: Crane Russak.

Fisher, Roger and William Ury. 1983. *Getting to Yes: Negotiating Agreement Without Giving In.* New York: Penguin Books.

Folk, Jerry. 1978. Peace Education—Peace Studies Programs: Towards an Integrated Approach. *Peace & Change* (Spring) 1, no. 1: 56-61.

Forcey, Linda Renine, ed. 1989. *Peace: Meanings, Politics, Strategies.* New York: Praeger.

Francis, Diana. 1990. Next Steps for the Peace and Justice Movement. *Fellowship* (October/November):12-13.

Freire, Paulo. 1970. *Pedagogy of the Oppressed.* New York: The Seabury Press.

Friesen, John, and Edith Elizabeth Wieler. 1988. New Robes for an Old Order: Multicultural Education, Peace Education, Cooperative Learning and Progressive Education. *Journal of Educational Thought* (April) 22, no. 1:46-56.

Fromm, Erich. 1976. *To Have or To Be?* New York: Bantam Books.

Gallie, W.B. 1978. *Philosophers of Peace and War.* Cambridge: Cambridge University Press.

Galtung, Johan. 1968. Entropy and the General Theory of Peace. In *IPRA Studies in Peace Research.* Proceedings of the International Peace Research Association Second Conference. Assen: Van Gorcum & Comp. N.V.

———. 1969. Violence, Peace, and Peace Research. *Journal of Peace Research* 6, no. 3:167-91.

———. 1985. Twenty-Five Years of Peace Research: Ten Challenges and Some Responses. *Journal of Peace Research* 22, no. 2:141-58.

———. 1988. The Next Twenty-five Years of Peace Research: Tasks and Prospects. In Wallensteen, Peter, ed. *Peace Research: Achievements and Challenges.* Boulder, CO: Westview Press.

———. 1988. Peace Studies in the U.S.: Six Deficits. *COPRED Peace Chronicle* (April):3-7.

Garcia, Gunnar. 1981. Androgyny and Peace Education. *Bulletin of Peace Proposals* 2:163-78.

Giddens, Anthony. 1985. Jurgen Habermas. In Skinner, Quentin, ed. *The Return of Grand Theory in the Human Sciences.* Cambridge: Cambridge University Press.

Giroux, Henry. 1981. *Ideology, Culture, and the Process of Schooling.* Philadelphia: Temple University Press.

Glissant, Edouard, editor-in-chief. 1986. *The Courier* (August) entire issue.

Glossop, Ronald J. 1977. The Peace Studies Program at Southern Illinois University at Edwardsville. *Peace & Change* (Spring) 4, no. 2:45-50.

Goebel, Ulrich, and Otto M. Nelson, eds. 1988. *War & Peace: Perspectives in the Nuclear Age.* Texas: Texas Tech University Press.

Goldstein, Joseph, and Jack Kornfield. 1987. *Seeking the Heart of Wisdom.* Boston and London: Shambhala.

Goozner, Merrill. 1990. Making peace through a war on methods of production. *Chicago Tribune.* 29 April. Sec. 7, p. 3.

Gordon, Haim. 1986. *Dance, Dialogue, and Despair: Existentialist Philosophy and Education for Peace in Israel.* Alabama: University of Alabama Press.

Gordon, Haim and Leonard Grob, eds. 1987. *Education for Peace: Testimonies From World Religions.* Maryknoll, NY: Orbis Books.

Gottlieb, Roger S., ed. 1989. *An Anthology of Western Marxism.* Oxford: Oxford University Press.

Green, Maxine. 1973. Teacher as Stranger. In O'Neill, William F. *Rethinking Education: Selected Readings in the Educational Ideologies.* Dubuque, IA: Kendall/Hunt.

Grof, Stanislov. 1988a. *The Adventure of Self-Discovery.* Albany: State University of New York Press.

_____. ed. 1988b. *Human Survival and Consciousness Evolution.* Albany: State University of New York Press.

Haas, Mary E. 1985. Considerations for Curriculum Development on Teaching War and Peace. *The Social Studies* (Nov-Dec) 76, no. 6:254-56.

Haavelsrud, Magnus. 1978. Peace Education. *International Peace Research Newsletter* 16 no. 1:32-43.

Haessly, Jacqueline. 1985. Peace-Making Goes to School. *The History and Social Science Teacher* (Spring) 20, no. 3-4:49-52.

Hanh, Thich Nhat. 1987. *Being Peace.* Berkeley, CA: Parallax Press.

Hanrieder, Wolfram F., ed. 1987. *Global Peace and Security: Trends and Challenges.* Boulder, CO: Westview Press.

Harle, Vilho, ed. 1987. *Essays in Peace Studies.* Aldershot, England: Avebury.

Harman, Willis. 1988. *Global Mind Change.* Indianapolis: Knowledge Systems, Inc.

Harris, Ian M. 1988. *Peace Education.* Jefferson, NC: McFarland & Company, Inc.

Henderson, George, ed. 1973. *Education for Peace: Focus on Mankind.* Washington D.C.: Association for Supervision and Curriculum Development.

Hentoff, Nat, ed. 1967. *The Essays of A.J. Muste.* Indianapolis: Bobbs-Merrill.

Hicks, David. 1986. Studying Peace: The Educational Rationale. Occasional paper no. 4, rev. ed. Lancaster, England: Centre for Peace Studies.

Hicks, David W., ed. 1988. *Education for Peace: Issues, Principles, and Practice in the Classroom.* London: Routledge.

Hodgkinson, Christopher. 1986. Peace Education: A Sophisticated Approach. *Education-Canada* (Winter) 26, no. 4:44-49.

Hollenbach, David. 1988. *Justice, Peace & Human Rights: American Catholic Social Ethics in a Pluralistic Context.* New York: Crossroads.

Howard, Michael. 1987. Peace Studies: The Hard Questions. In Kaye, Elaine, ed. *Peace Studies: The Hard Questions.* London: Rex Collings.

Howlett, Charles F. 1976. A Dissenting Voice: John Dewey Against Militarism in Education. *Peace & Change* (Spring) 3, no. 4:49-59.

———. 1977. *Troubled Philosopher: John Dewey and the Struggle for World Peace.* Port Washington, NY: Kennikat Press.

Hurst, John. 1987. A Pedagogy for Peace. In Carson, Terrance R., and Hendrik D. Gideonse, eds. *Peace Education and the Task for Peace Educators.* A World Council for Curriculum and Instruction Monograph.

Husen, Torsten. 1979. *The School in Question.* New York: Oxford University Press.

International Consultation on Peace Education and Research in Higher Education. 1986. *Higher Education in Europe* 11, no. 2:64-68.

IPRA Commission on Peace Education. 1978. Part II: Peace Education and the Violence of Knowledge. *International Peace Research Newsletter* 16, no. 3:32-73.

IPRA Studies in Peace Research. 1968. *Proceedings of the International Peace Research Association Second Conference.* Assen: Van Gorcum & Comp. N.V.

Jagger, Alison M. and Paula S. Rothenberg, eds. 1984. *Feminist Frameworks.* New York: McGraw-Hill, Inc.

Johnson, David M., ed. 1986. *Justice and Peace Education: Models for College and University Faculty.* Maryknoll, NY: Orbis Books.

Kaye, Elaine, ed. 1987. *Peace Studies: The Hard Questions.* London: Rex Collings.

Katz, Neil. 1986. Report on Graduate and Undergraduate Programs in Conflict Resolution. *Peace & Change* vol. 11, no. 2:80-95.

_____. 1989. Conflict Resolution and Peace Studies. *The Annals of the American Academy of Political and Social Science* (July) 504:14-21.

Kemp, Anita. 1985. Image of the Peace Field: An International Survey. *Journal of Peace Research* 22, no. 2:129-40.

Klare, Michael T. 1989. Peace Studies in the 1990s: Assessing Change in the Global War/Peace System. In Thomas, Daniel C., and Michael T. Klare, eds. *Peace and World Order Studies: A Curriculum Guide.* 5th ed. Boulder, CO: Westview Press.

Knudsen-Hoffman, Gene. 1990. True Reconciliation. *Fellowship* (January/February):9-10.

Kornfield, Jack. 1985. The Buddhist Path and Social Responsibility, *ReVision* 8 (Summer/Fall):63-67.

Kotkin, Joel. 1989. Is Peace Bad for Business? *Inc.* (August):33-34.

Krishnamurti, J. 1953. *Education and the Significance of Life.* San Francisco: Harper & Row.

_____. 1954. *The First and Last Freedom.* New York: Harper and Row.

_____. 1964. *Think on These Things.* New York: Harper & Row, Perennial Library.

_____. 1972. *You Are The World.* New York: Harper & Row.

_____. 1974. *Krishnamurti on Education.* New York: Harper & Row.

_____. 1979. *The Wholeness Of Life.* San Francisco: Harper & Row.

Lakey, George. 1987. *Powerful Peacemaking: A Strategy for a Living Revolution.* Philadelphia, PA: New Society Publishers.

Larson, Jeanne & Madge Micheels-Cyrus, comps. 1987. *Seeds of Peace.* Philadelphia: New Society Publishers.

Lebow, Richard Ned. 1988. Interdisciplinary Research and the Future of Peace and Security Studies. *Political Psychology* (Spring) 9, no. 3:522-24.

Levine, Stephen. 1979. *A Gradual Awakening.* New York: Anchor Books.

Lewis, Michael. 1978. *The Culture of Inequality.* Amherst: University of Massachusetts Press.

Lewis, Samuel. 1989. The U.S. Institute for Peace: A New Federal Role in Peace Education and Research. *COPRED Peace Chronicle* (January) 14, no. 1:5.

Lewy, Guenter. 1988. *Peace & Revolution: The Moral Crisis of American Pacifism.* Grand Rapids, MI: William B. Eerdmans Publishing Company.

Lifton, Robert Jay. 1987. *The Future of Immortality: And Other Essays for a Nuclear Age.* New York: Basic Books.

London, Herbert. 1985. Peace Studies—Hardly Academic. *New York Times.* 5 April. OpEd.

Lopez, George A. 1985. A University Peace Studies Curriculum for the 1990's, *Journal of Peace Research* 22, no. 2:117-28.

_____. 1989a. Conceptual Models for Curriculum Development. in Thomas, Daniel C., and Michael T. Klare, eds. *Peace and World Order Studies: A Curriculum Guide.* 5th ed. Boulder, CO: Westview Press.

_____. Special ed. 1989b. Peace Studies: Past and Future. *The Annals of the American Academy of Political and Social Science* (July) 504:61-71.

Matthews, Michael R. 1980. *The Marxist Theory of Schooling: A Study of Epistemology and Education.* New Jersey: Humanities Press.

Merton, Thomas, ed. 1965. *Gandhi on Non-Violence.* New York: New Directions Publishing Corporation.

McAllister, Pam, ed. 1982. *Reweaving the Web of Life: Feminism and Nonviolence.* Philadelphia: New Society Publishers.

McConaghy, Tom. 1986. Peace Education: A Controversial Issue? *Phi Delta Kappan* (November):248-49.

Montandon, Edmee, ed. 1983. Education for International Understanding, Peace, and Human Rights. *Bulletin of the International Bureau of Education* no. 226:5-83.

Montessori, Maria. 1943. *Peace and Education.* Adyar, Madras, India: The Theosophical Publishing House.

Mulch, Barbara Gooden. 1989. Institutionalizing Peace Studies in College Life. *The Annals of the American Academy of Political and Social Science* (July) 504:80-89.

Murray, Andrew. 1981. *Peace and Conflict Studies As Applied Liberal Arts: A Theoretical Framework for Curriculum Development.* Huntington, PA: Andrew Murray.

Nagler, Michael N. 1981. Peace as a paradigm shift. *Bulletin of the Atomic Scientist* (December) 37:49-52.

National Council of Teachers in English. 1940. *Educating for Peace.* New York: D. Appleton-Century Co.

Needleman, Jacob. 1980. *Lost Christianity: A Journey of Rediscovery.* San Francisco: Harper & Row.

O'Connell, James, and Adam Curle. 1985. *Peace with Work to Do: The Academic Study of Peace.* Great Britain: Berg Publishers Ltd.

O'Neill, William F. 1983. *Rethinking Education: Selected Readings in the Educational Ideologies.* Dubuque, IA: Kendall/Hunt.

Osborne, Ken. 1985. Peace Education and the Schools: What Can We Learn from History? *The History and Social Science Teacher* (Spring) 20, no. 3-4:33-41.

_____. 1987. Implementing Peace Education. *Learning, (Canada)* 4, no. 4:18-20.

Pagels, Elaine. 1981. *The Gnostic Gospels.* New York: Vintage Books.

Pikas, Anatol. 1974. *On Peace Education: The Concept of Positive Peace Meets Educational Necessities.* Uppsala, Sweden: Uppsala University, Dept. of Peace and Conflict Research.

Pirkl, Margaret, with Johanna Oriett, and Thomas J. Hamilton. 1983. An integrated approach to college peace education. *Momentum* (December) 14, no. 4:30-31.

Plaskin, Glenn. 1989. Trump: 'The People's Billionaire.' *Chicago Tribune.* 12 March. p. 1, 10.

Polkinghorne, Donald. 1983. *Methodology for the Human Sciences.* Albany: State University of New York Press.

Prasad, Devi. 1984. *Peace Education or Education for Peace.* New Delhi: Gandhi Peace Foundation.

Puri, Rashmi-Sudha. 1987. *Gandhi on War and Peace.* New York: Praeger.

Quester, George. 1989. International-Security Criticisms of Peace Research. *The Annals of the American Academy of Political and Social Science* (July) 504:98-105.

Quinney, Richard. 1988. Crime, Suffering, Service: Toward a Criminology of Peacemaking. *Quest* (Winter) 1, no. 2:66-75.

Rank, Carol. 1989. The Interdisciplinary Challenge of Peace Studies. In Thomas, Daniel C., and Michael T. Klare, eds. *Peace and World Order Studies: A Curriculum Guide.* 5th ed. Boulder, CO: Westview Press.

Read, Sir Herbert E. 1949. *Education for Peace.* New York: Charles Scribner's Sons.

Reardon, Betty A. 1988. *Comprehensive Peace Education: Educating for Global Responsibility.* New York: Teachers College Press.

_____. 1989. Pedagogical Approaches to Peace Studies. In Thomas Daniel C., and Michael T. Klare, eds. *Peace and World Order Studies: A Curriculum Guide.* 5th ed. Boulder, CO: Westview Press.

Renna, Thomas. 1980. Peace Education; an Historical Overview. *Peace and Change* 6, no. 1-2.

Rivage-Seul, Marguerite K. 1987. Peace Education: Moral Imagination and the Pedagogy of the Oppressed. *Harvard Educational Review* (May) 57, no. 2:153-69.

Roberts, Barbara. 1984. The Death of Machothink: Feminist Research and the Transformation of Peace Studies. *Women's Studies International Forum* 7, no. 4:195-200.

Ross, Nancy Wilson. 1981. *Buddhism: A Way of Life and Thought.* New York: Vintage Books.

Ryan, Howard, Angela McKee, and Chris Booth. 1987. Strategies for social change: a discussion of nonviolence. *Peace News* 11 December, 13-17.

Sakamoto, Yoshikazu, and Ruth Klaassen, eds. 1981. *Key Issues of Peace Research: Proceedings of the IPRA 9th Conference.* Orillia Ontario, Canada: IPRA.

Skinner, Quentin, ed. 1985. *The Return of Grand Theory in the Human Sciences.* Cambridge: Cambridge University Press.

Scott, Peter Dale. 1983. Peace, Power, and Revolution: Peace Studies, Marxism, and the Academy. *Alternatives* (New York), (Winter) 9, no. 3:359-61.

Scott, Peter Dale. 1987. Towards a Transpolitics: the Role of the Peace Educator. In Carson, Terrance R., and Hendrik D. Gideonse, eds. *Peace Education and the Task for Peace Educators.* A World Council for Curriculum and Instruction Monograph.

Senesh, Lawrence. 1975. Learning How to Live Peaceably. *Thresholds in Education* 1, no. 2:10-13.

Sharp, Gene. 1973. *The Politics of Nonviolent Action.* (3 volumes). Boston: Porter Sargent Publishers.

Shifferd, Kent. 1988. A Pedagogy of Peace. Unpublished paper given at the University of Wisconsin Conference on Education.

Simpson, Nan and Walter. 1988. Eating in Peace. *Fellowship* (September).

Singh, Karan. 1988. Transition to a New Consciousness. In Grof, Stanislov, ed. *Human Survival and Consciousness Evolution.* Albany: State University of New York Press.

Smoke, Richard, with Willis Harman. 1987. *Paths to Peace: Exploring the Feasibility of Sustainable Peace.* Boulder, CO: Westview Press.

Snitow, Ann. 1985. Holding the Line at Greenham: Being Joyously Political in Dangerous Times. *Mother Jones,* Feb./March, 1985:30-34, 39-47.

Somerville, John. 1975. *The Peace Revolution: Ethos and Social Process.* Westport, Connecticut: Greenwood Press.

Spretnak, Charlene. 1988. Dhamma at the Precinct Level. In Eppsteiner, Fred., ed. 1988. *The Path of Compassion: Writings on Socially Engaged Buddhism.* Berkeley: Parallax Press and the Buddhist Peace Fellowship. pp. 199-202.

Stanage, Sherman. 1989. Freire and Phenomenology: Person, Praxis, and Education for Infinite Tasks. 30 pgs.

Steeves, H. Leslie. 1987. Feminist Theories and Media Studies. *Critical Studies in Mass Communication,* 4, no. 2: 96-135.

Stephenson, Carolyn M. 1989. The Evolution of Peace Studies, In Thomas Daniel C., and Michael T. Klare, eds. 1989. *Peace and World Order Studies: A Curriculum Guide.* Fifth Edition. Boulder, Colorado: Westview Press. pp. 9-19.

Sweeney, Duane, ed. 1984. *The Peace Catalog.* Seattle, Washington: Press for Peace, Inc.

Struve, Jim. 1974. Peace Education: Experimental Grading. *Peace & Change,* Spring, 1974, II, no. 1:59-69.

Thelin, Bengt. 1988. Peace Education: Peace—Liberty—Development—Human Rights. *Western European Education,* Fall 1988, 20, no. 3:76-94.

Thomas, Daniel C. 1987. *Guide to Careers and Graduate Education in Peace Studies.* Massachusetts: University of Massachusetts at Amherst.

Thomas, Daniel C., and Michael T. Klare, eds. 1989. *Peace and World Order Studies: A Curriculum Guide.* Fifth Edition. Boulder, Colorado: Westview Press.

Tirman, John, ed. 1989. *Annual Review of Peace Activism.* Boston: Winston Foundation for World Peace.

Trump, Donald. 1987. *The Art of the Deal.* New York: Warner Books.

UNESCO. 1980. *Peace on Earth: A Peace Anthology.* Paris: United Nations Educational, Scientific and Cultural Organization.

Vaideanu, George. 1986. The Promotion of Peace Education in Higher Education Curricula. *Higher Education in Europe,* 1986, XI, no. 1:86-94.

Vasquez, John A. 1976. Toward a Unified Strategy of Peace Education. *Journal of Conflict Resolution.* December, 1976, XX, no. 4:707-28.

Vaughan, Frances. 1988. Transpersonal Vision. In Grof, Stanislov, ed. 1988b. *Human Survival and Consciousness Evolution.* Albany: State University of New York Press. pp. 9-17.

Vriens, Lennert, and Robert Aspelaugh. 1985. Peace Education as Alternating Between the Person and the Structure. *History and Social Science Teacher,* Spring, 1985, 20, no. 3-4:11-19.

Wagner, Richard V. 1988. Distinguishing between Positive and Negative Approaches to Peace. *Journal of Social Issues,* Summer, 1988, 44, no. 2:1-13.

Wallensteen, Peter. 1988a. The Origins of Peace Research. In Wallensteen, Peter, ed. 1988. *Peace Research: Achievements and Challenges.* Boulder, Colorado: Westview Press. pp. 7-29.

Wallensteen, Peter, ed. 1988b. *Peace Research: Achievements and Challenges.* Boulder, Colorado: Westview Press.

Walsh, Roger. 1984. *Staying Alive: The Psychology of Human Survival.* Boston: Shambhala Publications, Inc.

Washburn, Michael. 1971. Peace Education is Alive, But Unsure of Itself. *War/Peace Report* November, 1971, 11, no. 9:31-35.

Watkins, Mary. 1988. Imagination and Peace: On the Inner Dynamics of Promoting Peace Activism. *Journal of Social Issues*, 1988, vol. 44, no. 2, pp. 39-57.

Wehr, Paul and Michael Washburn. 1976. *Peace and World Order Systems*. Beverly Hills: Sage Publications.

Weigert, Kathleen Maas. 1989. Peace Studies as Education for Nonviolent Social Change. In Lopez, George A., special ed. 1989. Peace Studies: Past and Future. *The Annals of the American Academy of Political and Social Science*. July, 1989. Newbury Park: Sage Publications. pp. 37-47.

Weinberg, Arthur M. and Lila, eds. 1963. *Instead of Violence; Writings By the Great Advocates of Peace and Nonviolence Throughout History.* New York: Grossman Publishers.

Werner, Walt. 1985. Conceptions of Peace Education. *The History and Social Science Teacher*, 20, no. 3-4:29-32.

White, John. 1988. Jesus, Evolution, and the Future of Humanity. In Grof, Stanislov, ed. 1988b. *Human Survival and Consciousness Evolution*. Albany: State University of New York Press. pp. 119-34.

White, Ralph K. 1988. Specifics in a Positive Approach to Peace. *Journal of Social Issues*, Summer 1988, 44, no. 2:191-202.

Wiberg, Hakan. 1988. The Peace Research Movement. In Wallensteen, Peter, ed. 1988. *Peace Research: Achievements and Challenges*. Boulder, Colorado: Westview Press. pp. 30-53.

Wien, Barbara J. 1984. *Peace and World Order Studies: A Curriculum Guide*. Fourth Edition. New York: World Policy Institute.

Wilber, Ken. 1983. *Up From Eden*. Boulder: Shambhala Publications, Inc.

Wulf, Christoph, ed. 1974. *Handbook on Peace Education*. Frankfurt/Main—Oslo: International Peace Research Association (Education Committee).

Young, Nigel. 1981. Educating the Peace Educator. *Bulletin of Peace Proposals*, 1981, 12, no. 2.

_____. 1987. Some Current Controversies in The New Peace Education Movement: Debates and Perspectives. In Carson, Terrance R., and Hendrik D. Gideonse, eds. 1987. *Peace Education and the Task for Peace Educators*. A World Council for Curriculum and Instruction Monograph. pp. 26-34.

Zimmerman, Michael. 1988. The Incomplete Myth: Reflections on the 'Star Wars' Dimension of the Arms Race. In Grof, Stanislov, ed. 1988b. *Human Survival and Consciousness Evolution.* Albany: State University of New York Press. pp. 177-203.

Index

A

Abuse of women, 59
Adorno, Theodor, 36
Alker, Hayward, 37-38
Armed civic virtue, 29
Asia-Pacific region peace studies, 119
Associated Mennonite Biblical Seminaries, 113-14
Attitudes toward positive peace efforts, 6

B

Banking concept of education, 39
Boulding, Elise, 2-3, 4, 27, 48-49, 107, 110
Boulding, Kenneth, 2-3, 4, 20, 26, 27, 46
Bowles, Samuel, 154

Brethren, Church of the, 100, 115
Broad-based peace programs, 114-19, 125
Brock-Utne, Birgit, 8, 34, 59
Bulletin of the Peace Studies Institute and Program in Conflict Resolution, 115

C

Capitalism, 21, 52, 58, 60-67, 141
Catholic peace programs, 101
Center for Conflict Resolution (U. of Michigan), 2, 4, 27
Central American conflict studies, 6
Church of the Brethren, 100, 115
Cianto, David, 4
Civilian-based defense, 43
Classroom communication, and democracy, 17-18
College level peace studies programs, 4. *See also* Peace studies programs, review of
Colorado, University of (Boulder), 120
Columbia University Teachers College, 107-9
Conflict
    civilized, 20
    resolution and negotiation, 4, 27, 28
Conflict resolution peace study programs, 109-11, 123-24
Conflict studies, as attempt to achieve negative peace, 6
Conscientization, 39
Consciousness, transformation of, 41, 47-48, 49
Consortium for Peace Research, Education, and Development (COPRED), 4, 5, 101
Cooperatively owned businesses, 44
Creative imagination, 41
Critical peace research, 31
Critical Theory, 36-39, 68
Cuban missile crisis, 31
Cultural change, and transformationism, 41
Culture of Inequality, The, 61
Curriculum development, peace education grants, 5

parent disciplines, 10-12
transformationist approach, 129-43
    classroom atmosphere, 130-31
    cultural diversity of faculty, 133
    development of conceptual map of peace studies, 131
    experientially and theoretically based, 133
    interdisiplinary, 132
    introductory course, 133-34
    peace studies committee, 131
    proposed curriculum, 135-37
Czechosolvakian invasion, 31

D

Defense and Arms Control Studies Program, 111-12
Delegitimizing of war, 46-47
Dellinger, David, 57
Deming, Barbara, 58
Democracy/democratization, 16-21
    conflict and, 20
    equal respect between student and teacher, 19
    individualized education, 19
    open classroom communication, 17-18
    participatory nature of peace studies, 18
Dewey, John, 19, 24
Deutsch, Karl, 110
Dialogics, 39
Directory of Peace Studies Programs, 102
Direct violence, 7-8
Domination. *See* Patriarchy

E

Economic development, 6
Educating for Peace, 24-25
Educational liberal, 21. *See also* Liberalism
Edu-learner, 48

Ehrenreich, Barbara, 58, 66-67
Einstein, Albert, 56
Elementary school peace studies, 1-2
Elshtain, Jean Bethke, 26, 29
Empowerment, 39
Engels, Friedrich, 61
Environmental preservation, 6. *See also* Green Movement

F

Feminist positions on peace studies, 33-34
    socialist-feminism, 66-67
Fisher, Roger, 26, 28
Frankfurt School of Social Theory, 36-37
Freire, Paulo, 38, 39, 62
Fromm, Erich, 62
Funderburg Library, 116
Futurism, 48-49

G

Galtung, Johan, 2, 6, 8, 16, 32-33, 57, 110, 118
Gandhi, Mahatma, 41-42
Getting to Yes, 28
Gintis, Herbert, 65
Good citizenship education, 2, 25
Graduate programs in peace education, 104-6
    Associated Mennonite Biblical Seminaries, 113-14
    Columbia University Teachers College, 107-9
    MIT, 111-13
    Notre Dame, 116-18
    Syracuse University, 109-11
    University of Hawaii, 118-19
Greed, 62, 65. *See also* Capitalism
Greenham Common, 43-44
Green Movement, 44-45

H

Habermas, Jurgen, 36, 37-38
Hanh, Thich Nhat, 42
Harvard Negotiation Project, 28
Hawaii, University of, 118-19
Hermeneutics, 33
Hicks, David, 7, 19
Hinkelammert, Franz, 38
Historical overview, peace studies, 1-14
    branches of specialization, 3
    college and university level programs, 4
    defining peace, 5-9
    nuclear issues, 3-4
    overview of peace education efforts, 9-12
    pre-World War I, 1-2
    reactions to World Wars I and II, 2-3
    Vietnam War, 3
Historic Peace Churches, 100
Holistic learning, 41, 49
"Homo Noeticus," 142-43
Horkheimer, Max, 36
Howard, Michael, 8
Humanistic reform. *See* Liberationism
Hunger, 57, 63, 65
Hurst, John, 16

I

Ideologies of peace studies
    democracy and democratization, 16-21
    liberalism, 21-30, 50, 51
    liberationism, 22, 23, 30-40, 50, 51-52, 55-68
    transformationism, 22, 23, 40-49, 50-51, 53, 129-43
Imaging and futurism, 48-49
Individual action, 40
Individualism as educational objective, 24, 51

Individualized education, 19
Institute for International Peace Studies (Notre Dame), 116
Institute for Peace (U. of Hawaii), 118
Institute of Social Research (Frankfurt), 36
International education/world-global studies, 105, 107-9, 123
International and National Voluntary Service Training (U. of Colorado at Boulder), 120
International Peace Research Association (IPRA), 5, 32
International relations, and peace education, 2, 46
International Scholars Program (Notre Dame), 117
Internship, 18, 133
Inward quest for peace, 19-20

J

Journals, 147-48
Jung, Carl, 1

K

Katz, Neil, 110

L

Lakey, George, 42, 110
Lewis, Michael, 61
Liberalism, 21-30, 50, 51, 140
    conflict resolution approach, 28
    conservative interpretation, 24-25
    gradual reforms, 30
    individualism, 24
    liberal peace education, 26-27
    nuclear education, 28
    reform approach, 21
    war narrative, 29

Liberationism, 22, 23, 30-40, 50, 51-52
    see also Liberationist critique
    critical theory, 36-39
    feminist positions, 33-34
    Marxist and socialist perspectives, 34-37
    as outgrowth of 1960s events, 31
    reform approach, 30-31
    structural violence questions, 31-32
Liberationist critique, 55-68
    capitalism, 58, 60-67
    direct violence, 56-58
    patriarchy, 58-60
    socialist-feminism, 66-67
    structural violence, 58-67
Lopez, George, 2

M

Manchester College (Indiana), 2, 101, 114-16
Marcuse, Herbert, 36
Marx, Karl, 61
Marxism, 34-37, 52
Massachusetts Institute of Technology, 111-13
Maxwell School of Citizenship and Public Affairs, 109
Mennonite Church, 100, 113-14
Middle Eastern conflict studies, 6
Mill, John Stuart, 142
MIT, 111-13
Montessori, Maria, 24, 25-26
Muste, A.J., 56

N

Nagler, Michael, 45, 47
National Council of Churches, The, 8
National Council of English Teachers, 24
Nationalized health care, 44

Nation-state concept, 29, 30
Negative peace, 6-7, 25, 27, 32
Negotiation on the merits, 28
Neill, A.S., 24
Newtonian-Cartesian paradigm, 45, 67
New York Metropolitan Peace Studies Consortium, 121-22
Non-degree peace studies, 119-22
Nonviolence, 41-45, 53
Nonviolent revolution, 42-43
Norwich University, 119
Notre Dame, 116-18
Nuclear issues peace study programs, 3-4, 28, 106, 111-13, 124

O

Oppression of women, 58, 59-60

P

Paradigm shift, 45-49
Partial Test Ban Treaty, 31
Partipatory
    nature of peace studies, 18
    political processes, 6
Patriarchy, 58-60, 141
    elimination of patriarchal practices, 44
Peace, defining, 5-9
Peace and Change, 5
Peace and World Order Studies: A Curriculum Guide, 4
"Peace as a Paradigm Shift," 45
Peace Corps Preparatory Program (Norwich U.), 119
Peace encampment at Greenham Common, 43-44
Peace Studies in Graduate Education, 121
Peace Studies Institute, 114
Peace studies programs, review of, 99-127
    broad-based, 114-19, 125
        conflict resolution, 109-11, 123-24

       examples of representative programs, 104-6
       international education/world-global studies, 105, 107-9, 123
       major foci of, 102, 152
       non-degree granting efforts, 119-22
       nuclear issues, 106, 111-13, 124
       questionnaire, 149-50
       research background, 99-107
       spiritual base, 106, 113-14, 124-25
       statistics, 100-101
Pedagogy of the Oppressed, 39, 62
Phenomenology, 33
Political liberal, 21, *See also* Liberalism
Positional bargaining, 28
Positive peace, 6-7, 32
Positivism, 45-46
Praxis, 39, 41, 49
Presidential Commission on World Hunger, 57
Principled negotiation, 28
Problem-centered liberal approach to peace education, 29
Program for Conflict Resolution (Manchester College), 114-15
Program on Conflict Resolution (U. of Hawaii), 119
Program in Nonviolent Conflict and Change (Syracuse U.), 109-11
Program on the Analysis and Resolution of Conflict (Syracuse U.), 110, 111

Q

Quakers, 100

R

Racism, 59
Radical view of peace education. *See* Liberationism
Reardon, Betty, 47-48, 50, 107, 108, 110
Reform
       liberal view of, 21, 140
       liberationism view of, 30-31, 51

Research grants, 5
Respect between student and teacher, 19
Rivage-Seul, Marguerite, 38
Roberts, Barbara, 33-34
Rocco, Alfredo, 64

S

Scientific method, 27
Scott, Peter Dale, 17, 35
Self-realization, 21
Sharp, Gene, 42, 110
Shifferd, Kent, 18
Socialism, 43
Socialist-feminism, 66-67
Social justice, 6
Somerville, John, 60
Spirtual base peace programs, 106, 113-14, 124-25
Stable Peace, 27, 46
Structural violence, 6-8, 32
    capitalism, 58, 60-67
    liberationism and, 31-32, 58-67
    patriarchy, 58, 59-60
Syracuse University, 109-11

T

Teachers College, Columbia University, 107-9
Technical reason, 38
Third World poverty, 62-64
Thomas, Norman, 61
To Have or To Be?, 62
Toller, Ernst, 138
Transformationism, 22, 23, 40-49, 50-51, 53
    curricular implications of, 129-43
    delegitimization of war, 46-47
    educating emphasis, 47-48

       Green Movement, 44-45
       imaging and futurism, 48-49
       nonviolence, 41-45, 53
       paradigm shift, 45-49
Trump, Donald, 65

U

U.S. Institute of Peace (USIP), 5
University of Colorado at Boulder, 120
University of Hawaii, 118-19
University level peace studies programs, 4
University of Notre Dame, 116-18
Ury, William, 28

V

Values, 11, 17, 33
       transformationism and, 41
Vietnam War, 3, 31

W

Wallich, Henry C., 61
War
       delegitimizing of, 46-47
       liberationist critique, 56-58
       narrative, 29
Washburn, Michael, 4
Wehr, Paul, 4
White, John, 142
Women, domination of, 59-60
Women's peace encampment at Greenham Common, 43-44
Worker-owned businesses, 44
World education, 2

World-global studies, 105, 107-9, 123
World government, 43

Y

Young, Nigel, 10, 17, 110